GOD SENDS
HIS SON

THE STORY BIBLE SERIES

1. *God's Family* tells the story of creation, God's promises to Abraham's family, and the adventures of Joseph.

2. *God Rescues His People* tells about Israel's escape from Egypt, Moses and the Ten Commandments, and the wandering in the wilderness.

3. *God Gives the Land* tells the story of Joshua, the adventures of the judges, and the story of Ruth.

4. *God's Chosen King* tells about Samuel, Saul, and David, God's promises to David's family, and the Psalms.

5. *God's Wisdom and Power* tells about the glorious reign of Solomon, the wonderful works of Elijah and Elisha, and the Proverbs and the Song of Songs.

6. *God's Justice* tells the story of the prophets Amos, Hosea, Isaiah, and Jeremiah and their messages of God's judgment and mercy.

7. *God Comforts His People* tells about God's people in exile, their return to the land, and the adventures of Esther and Daniel.

8. *God Sends His Son* tells about God sending Jesus to set up his kingdom.

   Books 9 and 10 will complete the story of the New Testament.

Story Bible Series, Book 8

GOD SENDS HIS SON

Stories of God and His People from Matthew, Mark, Luke, and John

Retold by Eve B. MacMaster

Illustrated by James Converse

HERALD PRESS
Scottdale, Pennsylvania
Kitchener, Ontario
1986

Library of Congress Cataloging-in-Publication Data

MacMaster, Eve, 1942-
  God sends His Son.

  (Story Bible series ; bk. 8)
  1. Bible stories, English—N.T. Gospels.
I. Converse, James. II. Title. III. Series.
BS551.2.M29585   1986   226'.09505   86-18342
ISBN 0-8361-3420-6 (pbk.)

GOD SENDS HIS SON
Copyright © 1986 by Herald Press, Scottdale, Pa. 15683
    Published simultaneously in Canada by Herald Press,
    Kitchener, Ont. N2G 4M5. All rights reserved.
Library of Congress Catalog Card Number: 86-18342
International Standard Book Number: 0-8361-3420-6
Printed in the United States of America
Design: Alice B. Shetler

91 90 89 88 87 86 10 9 8 7 6 5 4 3 2 1

The Story of This Book

Several years ago I was looking for a Bible story book to read to my children. I wanted one that was complete, without tacked-on morals or a denominational interpretation. I wanted one that was faithful to the Bible and fun to read. I couldn't find what I was looking for.

With the encouragement of my husband, Richard MacMaster, I approached Herald Press with the idea of the series: a retelling of the whole Bible with nothing added and nothing subtracted, just following the story line through the Old and New Testaments.

The people at Herald Press were agreeable and enthusiastic and gave much valuable advice, especially general book editor Paul M. Schrock.

At his suggestion, I asked some academic and professional people in our community to check the stories for style and accuracy. Members of the advisory committee, who have kindly volunteered their time, include Bible professors George R. Brunk III, Ronald D. Guengerich, G. Irvin Lehman, and Kenneth Seitz; and childhood curriculum and librarian specialists Elsie E. Lehman and A. Arlene Bumbaugh.

I hope this series will lead its readers to the original, for no retelling is a substitute for the Bible itself. The Bible is actually a collection of books written over a long period of time in a variety of forms. It has been translated and retold in every generation because people everywhere want to know what God is like.

The main character in every story is God. The plot of every story is God's activity among his people: creating, saving, fighting, reigning, and doing works of wisdom and power, justice and mercy.

The first book in the series is *God's Family*. It tells stories about God the Creator.

The second book is *God Rescues His People*. It tells stories about God the Savior.

The third book is *God Gives the Land*. It tells stories about God the warrior.

The fourth book, *God's Chosen King*, tells stories about God the true king.

The fifth book, *God's Wisdom and Power*, tells stories about God, the source of wisdom and power.

The sixth book, *God's Justice*, tells stories about God the righteous judge.

The seventh book, *God Comforts His People*, tells stories about God's comforting mercy and promises.

With this book, *God Sends His Son*, we leave the world of the Old Testament and enter the world of the New. Here the promises of God come true in the person of Jesus of Nazareth. Here are the stories of the birth, life, and ministry of Jesus. He comes as bridegroom, teacher, and miracle worker. His coming forces everyone who meets him to make a decision. Is he really who he claims to be?

This volume is dedicated to the friends and teachers who have shown me by word and example how to be a disciple of Jesus.

—Eve MacMaster
Bridgewater, Virginia
Easter season 1986

Contents

Who Do You Say That I Am?

Map

The Author

The Coming
of the
Bridegroom

Waiting for the Anointed King

GOD had a plan. He was going to set up his kingdom and bring people of all nations under his rule. In his kingdom there would be peace and justice and a full, happy life for everyone.

God wanted to set up his kingdom because he loved the world he had made. The problem was, the people of earth didn't love God. They didn't want him to be their ruler.

Instead of obeying God, they preferred to obey all kinds of earthly kings and idols.

Instead of living in peace and loving each other,

they preferred lying, cheating, killing, and hating.

So God made a plan. He would choose a nation and teach them his ways. He would show them how to live. Through them, he would bless all nations.

God began by choosing Abraham to be the ancestor of his people. Then he built the nation of Israel from the family of Abraham. He rescued Israel from slavery in Egypt and gave them laws and commandments so they would know how to live.

God made a special agreement with Israel called the covenant. This covenant included God's promise to be Israel's God, to give them everything they needed, and to save them from their enemies. Israel promised to worship only the Lord God, and to live as he commanded.

God made other promises to his people. He promised that someone from the family of David, the king God chose for his people, would rule Israel forever.

God sent special messengers called prophets to tell his people how they should live and how he was planning to send an anointed king, a Messiah.

This Messiah, or Christ, would be from the family of David, and he would bring all nations under God's rule. He would be a human being, a Son of Man, but greater than any king or prophet. People of all nations, races, and lan-

guages would serve him. His rule would last forever.

For five hundred years kings from David's family ruled God's people. Then God allowed foreign armies to conquer Israel, to punish them for worshiping idols and breaking God's commandments.

For the next five hundred years Israel was ruled by foreigners—first the Assyrians, then the Babylonians, the Persians, the Greeks, and finally the Romans. The Romans set up Herod as king of the Jews, but the Jews, as Israel was called, hated Herod. They wanted their own king. They wanted to be free.

All these years they remembered God's promise to save them. God's promise was written in

the Scriptures, the Hebrew Bible, so God's people would remember his plan.

But when would God's promise come true? When would the Messiah come and rule over his people? When would the anointed king defeat their enemies and set them free?

2

The Angel of the Lord

Matthew 1; Luke 1

DURING the time when Herod was king of the Jews, there lived a priest named Zechariah. He and his wife, Elizabeth, were faithful people. They carefully followed all the commandments and teachings of the Lord their God. But they had no children, and they were both very old.

One day while Zechariah was taking his turn helping in the worship service at the temple in Jerusalem, something wonderful happened.

Zechariah entered the holy place inside the temple while the people stayed outside, praying.

He burned the sweet-smelling incense on a special altar, as a sign that the people's prayers were going up to heaven.

Suddenly an angel of the Lord appeared on the right side of the altar. When Zechariah saw the angel he was shocked, and fear came over him.

"Don't be afraid, Zechariah," said the angel. "Your prayers have been heard. Elizabeth will give birth to a son. You must name the child John, meaning 'the Lord has shown favor.' Your heart will be filled with joy, and many people will be glad that he was born. He will be great in the eyes of the Lord.

"He must never drink wine or beer, and from the moment of his birth he will be filled with the Holy Spirit. He will turn many Israelites back to the Lord their God. He will go ahead of the Lord, with the spirit and power of Elijah, the ancient prophet, and he will prepare the people to be ready for the coming of the Lord."

"How can I be sure of this?" Zechariah asked the angel. "I'm an old man, and my wife is old, too!"

"I am Gabriel," said the angel. "I stand in the presence of God. I have been sent to speak to you and to bring you this good news. Now listen. Because you haven't believed me, you'll lose the power of speech. You'll live in silence until the day the child is born. But you can be sure—at the proper time everything I've told you will come true!"

Meanwhile, the people outside the temple were waiting for Zechariah. They wondered why he was taking so long. When he finally came out, he couldn't say a word to them. He just stood there, making signs with his hands. They realized that he had seen a vision inside the temple.

Later, when Zechariah's time of service in the temple was over, he went home. Soon afterward his wife, Elizabeth, became pregnant.

"The Lord has done this!" thought Elizabeth, because she was very old. "Now people won't look down on me for never having had a child." For five months she kept to herself.

In the sixth month, the angel Gabriel was sent to a town in Galilee called Nazareth, to a young girl who was engaged to a man named Joseph. Joseph was a direct descendant of King David. The girl's name was Mary.

"Greetings, favored woman!" said the angel. "The Lord is with you!"

Mary was confused and surprised by these words. She wondered what the greeting could mean.

"Don't be afraid, Mary," said the angel. "God has favored you. You will become pregnant and give birth to a son. You must name him Jesus, meaning "savior." He will be great. He will be called the Son of the Most High God. The Lord God will give him the throne of his ancestor, David, and he will rule over the people of Israel forever. His reign will never end."

17

"How can this be possible?" asked Mary. "I'm still a virgin. I'm not married yet."

The angel answered, "The Holy Spirit will come upon you. The power of the Most High will overshadow you. The child will be holy, and he will be called the Son of God.

"Your cousin Elizabeth is also expecting a baby, even though she is very old. This woman whom no one thought could have children is now six months pregnant. Nothing is impossible for God!"

"I am the maidservant of the Lord!" said Mary. "As you have said, so let it happen."

Then the angel left her.

3

Mary's Song and Zechariah's Prophecy

Luke 1

SOON after the angel's announcement, Mary went to visit her cousin Elizabeth in the hill country of Judea. She entered the house and greeted Elizabeth, and when Elizabeth heard the greeting, the child inside her moved.

Elizabeth was filled with the Holy Spirit, and she cried out loud, "Blessed are you above all women, and blessed is your child! How honored I am that the mother of my Lord should visit me. I tell you, as soon as I heard your greeting, the child inside me leaped for joy! Blessed, indeed, is the woman who has believed, for the Lord's promise will come true!"

Then Mary praised God, saying:

My heart is full of praise
    for the greatness of the Lord.
My spirit is full of joy
    in God, my Savior.
For he has looked with favor on me,
    his servant, as lowly as I am.
From now on,
    all generations will call me blessed,
For the Lord, the Mighty One,
    has done wonderful things for me.
Truly, he has mercy on those who fear him
    in every generation.

What great deeds he has done!
How strong is the power of his right arm!
He has defeated the proud,
 the self-important.
He has pulled mighty rulers down
 from their thrones
 and has lifted up the lowly.
He has filled the hungry with good things,
 and the rich he has sent empty away.
He has come to the help of Israel, his servant,
 remembering the promises he made.
For he promised to show mercy
 to Abraham and his family, forever.

After this Mary stayed with Elizabeth for about three months, and then she returned to her own home.

When the time came for Elizabeth's baby to be born, she gave birth to a son. Her neighbors and relatives heard what God had done for her, and they shared her joy.

When the baby was eight days old, they went to circumcise him. This was the Jewish custom of marking baby boys as members of God's people.

They were going to name him Zechariah, after his father, but his mother objected. "No!" she said. "He must be named John."

"Nobody in your family has that name," they said, and they made signs to the baby's father to ask him what he wanted the child to be called.

Zechariah motioned for a writing tablet, and to everyone's amazement, he wrote the words, "His name is John."

Immediately, Zechariah was able to talk again, and he began to praise the Lord.

The neighbors were so impressed with what had happened that they told the whole story all over the hill country of Judea. Everyone who heard about it was amazed.

"What will this child become?" they asked. They could tell that the hand of the Lord was upon him.

Zechariah was filled with the Holy Spirit, and he spoke a message from God. First he said this about Mary's baby, Jesus, who wasn't yet born:

Praise the Lord, the God of Israel,
    for he has visited his people and set them free!
He has raised up for us a mighty Savior,
    in the family of his servant, David.
Long ago through his holy prophets
      the Lord promised to save us from our
          enemies,
      from the power of all who hate us.
He promised our ancestors that he would show
          mercy,
    and remember his holy covenant.
He made this promise to Abraham:
    to set us free from the power of our enemies—
Free to serve him without fear,
    to live in holiness and righteousness
    in his sight, all the days of our lives.

Then Zechariah spoke this prophecy about his son John:

And you, my child, will be called
    "the prophet of the Most High."
You will go ahead of the Lord,
    to prepare the way for his coming.
You will give his people knowledge of salvation,
    through the forgiveness of their sins.
For the heart of our God is full of tender mercy;
      he sends the first light from heaven to shine
      upon us,
And to shine on people who live in darkness,
    under the cloud of death;
And to guide our feet
    into the path of peace.

As John grew up, he became strong in the Spirit. He lived in the wilderness until the day he appeared publicly to the people of Israel.

4

Good News!

Matthew 1; Luke 2

JOSEPH didn't know what to do. He was so worried, he thought about his problem in his sleep. Should he go ahead and marry the girl he was engaged to, or should he break off the engagement? He knew Mary was pregnant, and the baby wasn't his.

Joseph was a decent man. He didn't want Mary to be publicly disgraced. Perhaps he would just break the engagement quietly, he thought.

While Joseph was turning this over in his mind, an angel of God appeared to him in a dream.

"Joseph, son of David!" said the angel. "Don't be afraid to take Mary as your wife, for she has become pregnant by the Holy Spirit. She will give birth to a son, and you must name him Jesus, because he will save his people from their sins."

Joseph woke up and did as the angel said. He took Mary home with him to be his wife.

A few months later Joseph and Mary left Nazareth in Galilee and went to the town of Bethlehem in Judea. Bethlehem was the town of Joseph's ancestor, David. Joseph was going there to register, because the Roman emperor, Augustus Caesar, had ordered his officials to count all the people in the empire. While Joseph and Mary were in Bethlehem, the time came for Mary's baby to be born.

Mary gave birth to a son, and she wrapped him in tight bands of cloth called swaddling clothes. Then she laid him in a manger, because there was no room for them at the inn.

In the countryside near Bethlehem there were shepherds out in the fields keeping watch over their flocks of sheep through the night. Suddenly the angel of the Lord stood in front of them, and the glory of the Lord shone around them. The shepherds were terrified.

"Don't be afraid," said the angel. "I have good news for you. Great joy is coming for everyone. Today in the city of David a Savior has been born for you. He is the Messiah, the Lord!

"This will be a sign for you: you will find the baby wrapped in swaddling clothes and lying in a manger."

All at once a great company of the heavenly army appeared with the angel, praising God and singing:

> Glory to God in the highest heaven,
> and on earth, his peace
> for people whom he favors.

After the angels left and went back into heaven, the shepherds said to each other, "Come! Let's go straight to Bethlehem and see this thing which the Lord has made known to us."

They hurried off and found Mary and Joseph and the baby. The baby was wrapped in swaddling clothes and lying in a manger.

When they saw the child, the shepherds repeated what the angel had told them. Everyone who heard about it was amazed.

Mary listened and kept all these things in her heart, thinking about them over and over.

The shepherds returned to the fields, glorifying and praising God for what they had seen and heard. Everything had happened exactly as the angel had said.

When the baby was eight days old, Mary and Joseph went to circumcise him, according to the Jewish custom. They named him Jesus, as they had been told.

When the baby was forty days old, they took him to Jerusalem, to present him to the Lord in the temple. This was another Jewish custom, to offer a sacrifice for a firstborn child. According to the law of Moses, a lamb was offered if the parents could afford it. If they couldn't afford a lamb, they offered two pigeons instead. Joseph and Mary offered pigeons.

At that time in Jerusalem there was a man named Simeon, a good and pious man who was waiting for God to free Israel. The Holy Spirit was with him, and it had been revealed to him that he would not die until he had seen the Lord's anointed king.

Simeon now came to the temple, guided by the Holy Spirit. When Mary and Joseph brought the baby Jesus in, Simeon took the baby in his arms and praised God, saying:

Now, Lord, you have set me, your servant, free—
    free to go in peace, as you have promised.
For my eyes have seen the Savior,
    whom you have prepared for the whole world
    to see.
He will be a light to show truth to foreign nations,
    and to bring glory to your people, Israel.

Joseph and Mary were amazed by what Simeon was saying. Then Simeon blessed them and said to Mary, "This child will be a sign from God that many people will reject. You'll be hurt, too. Many people in Israel will stand or fall because of him, and the secret thoughts of many will be revealed."

There was also in Jerusalem a prophetess named Anna. She was an old woman who had been a widow for many years. She never left the temple area, but worshiped God day and night.

Just as Simeon was saying these things about Jesus, Anna came by. She began to praise God publicly, speaking about the child to everyone who was waiting for God to free Jerusalem.

5

Visitors from the East

Matthew 2; Luke 2

S OME months after Jesus was born astrologers from the East arrived in Jerusalem. In those days in the ancient world astrologers were respected for their wisdom. They carefully studied the stars and planets and other knowledge.

These wise men had traveled all the way from Babylonia or Persia. When they arrived in Judea they asked, "Where is the child who has been born to be king of the Jews? We have seen his star rising, and we have come to bow down before him."

When King Herod heard about this he was very upset and so were all the important men in Jerusalem.

The king called a meeting of the chief priests and scribes, who were the religious leaders of the Jews.

"Where is the Messiah to be born?" he asked them.

"In the town of Bethlehem in Judea," they answered. "This is what the prophet wrote," and they quoted the prophet Micah:

Bethlehem in the land of Judah,
   you are far from least in Judah.
For from you will come a ruler
   to be the shepherd of my people, Israel.

Herod invited the wise men to meet with him in private. He learned from them the exact time the star had appeared, and then he sent them to Bethlehem.

"Go and find out all about the child," he said. "When you have located him, report to me so I can go and bow down before him, too."

As the wise men went on their way, they saw the same star going ahead of them. The sight of the star filled them with joy. They followed it until it stopped over the house where the little child and his family were living.

They went into the house. When they saw the child and his mother, they bowed down before him. Then they opened their treasures and offered him gifts of gold, incense, and myrrh.

Later the wise men were warned in a dream not to go back to Herod, and so they returned home another way.

After they had gone, an angel of the Lord appeared to Joseph in a dream.

"Rise up," said the angel. "Take the child and his mother and escape with them to Egypt. Stay there until I tell you, for Herod will search for the child in order to kill him."

Joseph got up and took the child and his

mother and left for Egypt that same night. They stayed in Egypt for some time.

When Herod realized that the wise men had tricked him, he was furious. He sent some men to Bethlehem with orders to massacre all the baby boys two years old and younger. He had figured the age from what the wise men had told him.

Soon after this Herod died, and the angel of the Lord appeared in a dream to Joseph in Egypt.

"Rise up," said the angel. "Take the child and his mother and return with them to the land of Israel, for the men who wanted to kill the child are dead."

Joseph got up and took the mother and child and returned to the land of Israel. They settled in Nazareth, in Galilee.

As Jesus grew up, he became big and strong and full of wisdom, and God's blessing was upon him.

6

Jesus in His Father's House

Luke 2

EVERY year Jesus' parents went to Jerusalem for the feast of the Passover, the most important of all the yearly religious holidays. Every Jewish family tried to go to Jerusalem at Passover time to pray at the temple, the house of God.

When Jesus was twelve years old, his family went as usual. After the feast was over, they started for home, but Jesus stayed behind in Jerusalem. His parents didn't know this.

Mary and Joseph thought he was with the

group they were traveling with, and they went on for a whole day without him. When they found out that he was missing, they began to look for him among their friends and relatives. When they couldn't find him, they returned to Jerusalem to search for him there.

On the third day they found Jesus in the temple, sitting in the middle of the scribes. The scribes were men who studied the law of Moses (the Torah) and the writings of the ancient prophets. They were experts in these Hebrew Scriptures (the Jewish Bible). They read and studied the commandments and promises of God and taught them to the people.

Jesus listened to the scribes and asked them questions. He joined their discussions, and everyone who heard him was amazed by his understanding and the answers he gave.

Mary and Joseph were shocked to see Jesus there among the religious teachers.

"My son," said his mother, "why have you treated us like this? Your father and I have been terribly worried. We've looked everywhere for you!"

"Why are you looking for me?" Jesus asked. "Didn't you know that I must be in my Father's house?" They didn't understand what he meant. They didn't understand that he was talking about his heavenly Father.

Then Jesus returned to Nazareth with Joseph and Mary and was obedient to them. His mother kept all these things in her mind and thought about them, over and over.

Jesus kept on growing in mind and body, and in favor with God and the people who knew him.

7

A Voice Crying in the Wilderness

Matthew 3; Mark 1; Luke 3; John 1

JOHN, the son of Zechariah and Elizabeth, lived in the wilderness away from the towns and cities of Judea. Like the ancient prophet Elijah, John wore rough clothes made of animal skins. He lived on locusts and honey and never drank wine or beer.

Then the word of God came to John and he repeated God's message to the people. He preached across the Jordan River from Jericho, at the place where Elijah had been taken up to heaven. He preached like an ancient prophet, calling the people to turn from their sins and obey the Lord their God.

"Repent!" he cried. "Turn from your sins and be baptized, and God will forgive you. For the kingdom of God is near!"

People from the city of Jerusalem and from all over Judea went out to the wilderness to hear John's preaching. They paid attention to the message and turned back to the Lord. They confessed their sins, and John baptized them in the Jordan River.

Baptism was a sign that they had turned from their sins and accepted God's forgiveness. It was the custom of the Jews to wash as a sign of being clean in the eyes of God. This baptism of water was a sign that the people understood God's message and wanted to be clean.

John told the people, "If you've really turned from your sins, then show it by changing your behavior. Don't just say that everything's all right because Abraham's your ancestor. I tell you, God can make descendants of Abraham from these stones!"

It wasn't enough to be born into God's people. God wanted his people to obey his commandments and follow his teaching. Soon, warned John, God himself was coming to judge them. Those who didn't change their behavior would be punished.

"Then what should we do?" asked the people.

John answered, "Whoever has two shirts

should share with the person who has none. Whoever has food should do the same."

Some tax collectors came to be baptized. Tax collectors were hated because they worked for the Romans and became rich by cheating the people.

"Teacher," they asked, "what should we do?"

"Collect nothing extra for yourselves," John answered. "Just take what's allowed."

Then some soldiers asked, "What about us? What should we do?"

John answered, "Stop your bullying and your blackmail. Be content with your pay."

The people were excited by John's preaching. They could tell that he was a messenger from God. They began to wonder who he was. Could John be the Messiah, the anointed king they were waiting for?

The religious leaders in Jerusalem were also wondering about John. They sent some priests to ask him who he was.

John answered them plainly, "I am not the Messiah."

"Well, then," they said, "who are you—Elijah? We expect Elijah to return."

"No."

"Are you the prophet that Moses said would come?"

"No."

"Then who are you? We must take an answer to Jerusalem. What do you say for yourself?"

John answered with a quote from the prophet Isaiah: "I am

> A voice crying in the wilderness,
>   'Prepare a way for the Lord!
>   Clear a straight path for him!' "

But the messengers from Jerusalem weren't satisfied with John's answer. "If you're not the Messiah or Elijah or the prophet Moses said would come, then why do you baptize?" they asked.

"I baptize with water, for repentance," answered John. "People hear my preaching and turn from their sins. But there is someone coming after me who is greater than I am. I'm not

good enough to untie his sandals. I've baptized with water, but he'll baptize with the Holy Spirit and with fire.

"When he comes, he'll be like a farmer at harvesttime, gathering his crop. He'll separate the good grains of wheat from the useless chaff. He'll put the grain into his barn, but he'll burn the chaff in an everlasting fire."

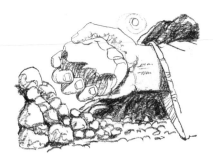

8

Jesus Is Baptized and Tempted

Matthew 3—4; Mark 1; Luke 3—4

WHEN John began to preach, Jesus was about thirty years old. He came from Nazareth in Galilee to the place where John was baptizing, on the east side of the Jordan River. After all the people had been baptized, Jesus came to be baptized, too.

"Do you come to me?" asked John, trying to stop him. "I'm the one who needs to be baptized by you."

"Let it be," said Jesus. "This is what we must do to fulfill all the requirements of God's plan."

41

Then John baptized him. As Jesus came up out of the water, heaven opened and the Holy Spirit came down like a dove and rested upon him.

A voice came from heaven, saying, "This is my beloved Son, and my favor rests on him."

After his baptism, Jesus was led by the Spirit through the wilderness. There he stayed for forty days, fasting. All that time he had nothing to eat, and at the end of the forty days he was starving.

Then Satan came to Jesus and tempted him. "If you are the Son of God," he said, "order these stones to turn into loaves of bread."

Jesus answered, "Scripture says:

> People don't live just on food,
> but on every word that comes
> from the mouth of God."

Then Satan took Jesus to the holy city of Jerusalem and set him on the highest part of the temple.

"If you are the Son of God," he said, "throw yourself down. For Scripture says:

God will order his angels to take care of you;
they will support you in their arms,
and you won't even stub your toe."

"Yes," answered Jesus, "and Scripture also says:

You must not put the Lord your God to the test."

Then Satan took Jesus up to a very high mountain and showed him the kingdoms of the world in their glory.

"I'll give you all this," he said. "You can have everything that goes with it—the wealth and power of these kingdoms. It has all been put into my hands, and I can give it to anyone I please. Just bow down before me, and it will all be yours."

"Go away, Satan!" said Jesus. "Scripture says:

You must worship the Lord your God,
and him only must you serve."

Then Satan was finished testing Jesus, and he left him for a while, and angels came and took care of Jesus.

9

The Coming
of the Bridegroom

John 1—3

JESUS returned to the place where John was baptizing, and he found John standing there with two of his disciples;

"Look!" John called out as Jesus walked by. "There is the Lamb of God!"

John's disciples heard him say this, and they left him and followed Jesus.

Jesus turned and saw them following him and asked them, "What are you looking for?"

"Teacher," they said, "where are you staying?"

"Come and see," he answered.

They went and saw where he was staying, and they remained with him the rest of the day. It was about four o'clock in the afternoon.

One of the two men who had followed Jesus was Andrew. The first thing Andrew did was find his brother Simon. (This was the same Simon who was later called Peter.)

"We have found the Messiah!" Andrew told Simon, and he took his brother to Jesus.

The next day Jesus met Philip, a man from Bethsaida in Galilee, Andrew and Simon's hometown.

"Follow me," he said. And Philip followed him.

Then Philip went to find Nathanael. "We have met the man described in the Law and the Prophets!" he said. "He's Jesus, son of Joseph, from Nazareth!"

"Nazareth!" scoffed Nathanael. "Can anything good come from Nazareth?"

"Come and see for yourself," answered Philip.

"Look!" said Jesus when he saw Nathanael coming. "Here's a true Israelite. There's nothing phony about him!"

"How do you know me?" asked Nathanael.

Jesus answered, "Before Philip called you, I saw you under the fig tree."

"Teacher!" said Nathanael. "You are the Son of God! You are the king of Israel!"

Jesus answered, "Do you have faith because I told you that I saw you under the fig tree? I promise you, you're going to see even greater things than that!"

After he gathered these first followers, Jesus led them into Judea. They became his disciples, learning from him as students learn from a teacher. They called him "rabbi," meaning teacher, and they went with him everywhere.

In Judea they baptized some people, and the disciples of John were jealous.

"Teacher," they said to John, "that man who was with you on the other side of the Jordan— the one you've been talking about—well, now he's baptizing, and the people are going to him!"

When he heard this, John wasn't jealous. He

explained to his disciples why Jesus was more important than he was, and how Jesus was more than just another teacher.

"Don't you remember?" he said. "I told you I'm not the Messiah. I'm the one who has been sent to prepare the people for the Messiah. It's like a bridegroom and his best man. Jesus is the groom, and I'm the groom's friend who prepares everything for him. The groom takes the bride.

"Jesus is like the groom and Israel is the bride. I'm happy to be the groom's friend. I'm glad just to hear his voice. For Jesus must become greater and greater, while I must become less and less important."

A short time after this, Jesus and his disciples went to Galilee, and Jesus worked a miracle at a friend's wedding. This was the first sign that he gave to show his glory, and it caused his disciples to believe in him.

Jesus and his friends were invited to a wedding feast in the town of Cana. Jesus' mother was one of the guests. When the wine was all gone, she said to him, "They have no wine left."

"Woman," he said, "what does that have to do with me? My time has not yet come."

His mother said to the servants, "Do whatever he tells you."

Six stone water jars were standing there, the kind the Jews used for religious washing. Each jar held about twenty gallons.

"Fill the jars with water," ordered Jesus, and

they filled them to the brim. "Now," he said, "pour some water out and take it to the steward in charge of the feast."

They did, and when they gave the steward the water—which had now turned to wine—he tasted it. He had no idea where it had come from. Only the servants who had poured the water knew that Jesus had changed the water to wine.

The steward called the bridegroom over and said, "Everyone serves the best wine first. After the guests have been drinking a while, they usually serve cheap wine. But you have kept the best for now!"

Jesus Announces
the Kingdom
of God

10

"The Kingdom of God Is Near!"

Matthew 4, 8, 13; Mark 1, 6; Luke 3—4; John 4

AFTER King Herod died, his kingdom was divided among his three sons. The oldest, Archelaus, ruled Judea and Samaria until the Romans replaced him with their own governor, Pontius Pilate. Another son, Philip, ruled Iturea, and a third son, Herod Antipas, ruled Galilee.

Herod Antipas was a wicked man who committed many crimes. John the Baptist criticized Herod publicly, and when Herod married Herodias, his brother's wife, John said this was against the law.

Then Herod added another crime to all the rest by locking John up in prison. When this news reached Jesus, he decided to stay away from Jerusalem and Judea. He settled in Capernaum, a town on the shore of the large lake called the Sea of Galilee.

The power of the Holy Spirit was with him, and he began to preach to the people. "The time has come!" he announced. "The kingdom of God is near. The rule of God has arrived. Repent, turn from your sins, and believe this good news!"

Jesus taught in the synagogue at Capernaum. The Jews gathered in their synagogues every week on the Sabbath day to praise the Lord with psalms and prayers and Scripture reading.

One Sabbath day as Jesus was teaching in the synagogue, a man with an unclean spirit screamed at him.

"Ha!" he cried. "What do you want with us, Jesus of Nazareth? Have you come here to destroy us? I know who you are. You're the Holy One of God!"

"Be quiet!" Jesus ordered the unclean spirit. "Come out of him."

The demon threw the man down and left him, screaming loudly.

"What's this?" the people asked in amazement. "Is this a new kind of teaching? This man commands unclean spirits to come out, and they obey him!" And they told the news about Jesus all over Galilee.

Jesus left the synagogue and went to the house of Simon and Andrew, where he found Simon's mother-in-law in bed with a high fever. As soon as Jesus arrived, they asked him to help. He went to her and touched her and commanded the fever to leave her. It left immediately, and she got up and began to serve them.

That evening after sunset people came to the house where Jesus was staying. They brought their friends to be healed of all kinds of sickness. The whole town was there, gathered in front of the house and crowding around the door. Jesus laid his hands on the sick people one by one, healing them and driving out demons.

Early the next morning, before the sun was up, he went to a deserted place to pray. The crowds came after him, and his friends went looking for him.

"Everyone's searching for you," said Simon and his friends when they found him.

The people begged Jesus not to leave, but he answered, "I must preach the good news of God's rule in other towns, too. That is what I was sent for."

Jesus traveled all over Galilee, teaching and preaching the good news about the kingdom of heaven and healing the people of every kind of disease. They were amazed by the power of his teaching. He didn't sound like the scribes, who were always quoting other teachers. Jesus spoke with authority.

When he arrived in Nazareth, his hometown, he went to the synagogue on the Sabbath. He stood up to read the Scriptures, and they handed him the scroll of the prophet Isaiah.

Jesus unrolled the scroll and found the place where it was written:

The Spirit of the Lord is upon me,
    for he has anointed me.
He has sent me to preach good news to the poor,
    to announce liberty to the captives,
To bring sight to the blind,
    to set the prisoners free,
And to announce that the time has come
    when the Lord will show favor to his people.

Then Jesus rolled the scroll up and handed it back to the attendant and sat down. All eyes in the synagogue were staring at him.

"Today, as you sit and listen," he said, "this passage of Scripture is coming true."

The people didn't expect Jesus to talk like this. "Where did he get such wisdom and power?" they asked.

"Isn't he the carpenter, the son of Mary and Joseph the carpenter?"

"Aren't his brothers James, Joseph, Judas, and Simon?"

"His sisters live right here in Nazareth."

They refused to accept him. They remembered him as an ordinary person, and they were offended by what he was saying.

Jesus answered them, "You want me to work miracles here as I did in Capernaum. I tell you, no prophet is recognized in his hometown. The prophet Elijah wasn't sent to the widows of Israel—though there were many—but to a foreign widow. The prophet Elisha didn't heal the lepers of Israel—though there were many—but he healed Naaman the Syrian."

When the people in the synagogue heard this, they were furious. They jumped up and grabbed Jesus and dragged him out of town. They took him to the edge of a cliff and were about to throw him over, but he walked through the crowd and went on his way.

11

The Amazing Power of Jesus

Matthew 4, 8, 9; Mark 1—2; Luke 5; John 5

JESUS taught in the synagogues, but he also taught outdoors, in the fields and beside the lake. Huge crowds came to hear him.

One day while he was standing beside the Sea of Galilee, teaching the people, the crowd was pressing so close to him, he had no place to stand. He noticed two boats pulled up onto the beach, fishermen's boats left there while the fishermen cleaned their nets.

Jesus stepped into Simon Peter's boat and asked him to push off a little distance from the shore. Then he sat down and taught the people from the boat.

When he was finished, he said to Simon, "Push the boat further out into the deep water, and let down your nets for a catch of fish."

"Teacher," said Simon, "we worked hard all night long and we didn't catch a thing. But if you say so, I'll let down the nets."

Simon and the other fishermen let down the nets, and they caught so many fish that the nets began to tear. They motioned to their partners in the other boat to come and help them. Then they loaded both boats so full of fish, they almost sank.

When he saw this, Simon was so filled with wonder, he dropped to his knees in front of Jesus.

"Leave me, Lord," he said, "for I am a sinful man!

The other fishermen were also amazed by the huge catch of fish they had pulled in. These were James and John, Simon's fishing partners.

"Don't be afraid," Jesus said to them. "Follow me, and you'll become fishers of men. You'll catch people!"

James and John brought their boats back to shore, and then they left everything and followed Jesus. They went with him and the other disciples to the towns of Galilee, where he taught the people and healed them of their diseases.

The power of God was with Jesus to heal the people, even those with terrible diseases like leprosy. People everywhere wanted to be close to him and touch him, for they heard about the wonderful things he was doing.

One day, when he was teaching inside a house, so many people were crowding around him that no one else could get in. They couldn't even reach the front door.

Four men arrived at the house carrying a paralyzed man on a stretcher. Because of the crowd, they couldn't bring their sick friend in and lay him in front of Jesus. So they went up onto the flat roof of the house and made a hole

over the place where Jesus was teaching. Then they lowered the paralyzed man on his mat down through the roof and right into the middle of the room.

When Jesus saw how much faith they had, he said to the man, "My son, your sins are forgiven."

Some of the scribes who were in the crowd were annoyed when he said this. They thought to themselves, "How dare this man say such a thing? It's an insult to God. Only God can forgive sins!"

Jesus knew what they were thinking, and he said to them, "Why are you thinking such things? Is it easier to say to this paralyzed man, 'Your sins are forgiven,' or so say, 'Stand up and walk?' " Then he added, "I'll show you that the Son of Man has power on earth to forgive sins."

He turned to the paralyzed man and said, "I tell you, stand up. Pick up your mat, and go home!"

The man stood up in front of all the people, picked up his mat, and walked out. He went home, praising God.

The people were amazed and filled with wonder. They praised God, saying, "We've never seen anything like this!"

12

What Does God Want?

Matthew 9, 12; Mark 2—3; Luke 5—6

AS JESUS was walking along the shore of the Sea of Galilee, he saw a man named Matthew sitting at his desk in the tax collector's office.

"Follow me," said Jesus, and Matthew got up and followed him.

Later on Matthew gave a big party at his house, with Jesus as the guest of honor. Among the other guests were many tax collectors and sinners. A lot of people with bad reputations were following Jesus, and they came and sat with him and his disciples.

The scribes were shocked. They expected Jesus to act the way they did and stay away from bad people.

The strictest, most religious of all these scribes were the Pharisees. They were the popular religious leaders who taught the common people in the synagogues. They not only followed the whole law of Moses, they also followed hundreds of other rules that had been worked out since the time when the Hebrew Scriptures were written.

These Pharisees were sure that God was pleased with them. They were proud of themselves, and they enjoyed having other people look up to them. They were proud of their ancestors, proud of belonging to God's chosen people, Israel. They looked down on all sinners and foreigners.

Now when the Pharisees saw Jesus eating with sinners, they said to his disciples, "Why does your teacher eat and drink with tax collectors and sinners?"

Jesus overheard this question. "It's not the healthy people who need a doctor," he answered, "but sick people! I haven't come for those who are already good, but for sinners."

Then he said to them, "Go and look in the Scriptures for the meaning of this teaching," and he quoted the prophet Hosea:

What God wants is loving-kindness, not sacrifices.

The Pharisees were surprised and annoyed by

this answer. Even though the ancient prophets had said over and over that God wanted loving-kindness more than strict religious behavior, they did just the opposite. They were careful to follow every little rule, but they paid no attention to the most important teaching of Moses and the prophets.

Jesus was always surprising people. He didn't act the way they expected religious teachers to act. Most people expected him to make a great show of fasting and praying in public, to follow strict rules, and to go around looking gloomy.

"Why don't your disciples fast?" they asked him. Going without food was something they expected from really religious people. "The disciples of John the Baptist and the disciples of the Pharisees are always fasting."

Jesus answered, "Would you expect wedding guests to look gloomy and fast while the bridegroom was still at the wedding feast? My disciples will fast when I am taken away from them."

Jesus was bringing something new and surprising, but they preferred the old. The Pharisees kept criticizing him.

One Sabbath day Jesus and his disciples were walking through some wheat fields, and the disciples were hungry. They began to pick the wheat, and rub it in their hands, and eat it.

"Look!" said the Pharisees to Jesus when they saw this. "Your disciples are doing something

61

that our law says is forbidden on the Sabbath!"

Jesus answered, "Don't you remember the story about David and his followers? When they were hungry, David went into the house of God and took the offering bread and ate it and gave it to his men. That bread was reserved for the priests, but they ate it anyway.

"I tell you," he said, "if you understood the teaching of the prophets, you wouldn't be so quick to criticize. For

What God wants is loving-kindness, not sacrifices.

And the Son of Man is ruler, even of the Sabbath!"

On the same Sabbath day Jesus went into a

synagogue and taught the people, and the Pharisees followed him and watched him.

In that synagogue there was a man with a withered hand. The Pharisees wondered whether Jesus would heal the man on the Sabbath, so they could accuse him of breaking the law.

Jesus knew what they were thinking. "Is it right to do good on the Sabbath, or to do harm?" he said. "To save life or to destroy it?"

No one in the synagogue answered him. Jesus looked at the people with anger and sadness because they were so stubborn. Then he said to the man with the withered hand, "Stretch out your hand!"

He did, and his hand was healed instantly.

The Pharisees left the synagogue in an angry fit. They were so mad, they began to talk about getting rid of Jesus.

13

Two Surprising Conversations

John 2—4

JESUS went to Jerusalem to celebrate the yearly Passover. While he was there, he worked miracles, and many people believed in him.

One night a Jewish leader named Nicodemus came to see Jesus. Nicodemus was a Pharisee and a member of the ruling council of the Jews.

"Teacher," said Nicodemus, "we know that you have been sent by God, because nobody could do the miracles you do unless God was with him."

"I tell you the truth," said Jesus. "No one can see God's kingdom without being born from above."

"How can a grown man be born again?" asked Nicodemus. "Can he go back into his mother's womb and be born all over again?"

"I tell you the truth," said Jesus. "No one can enter the kingdom of God without being born of water and the Spirit. A person is born physically from parents, but spiritually from the Spirit."

"How can such things be possible?" asked Nicodemus.

"What?" said Jesus. "Do you mean to say that you're a respected teacher in Israel and you don't understand?"

Then Jesus said something even more surprising. "God so loved the world that he gave his only Son, so that everyone who believes in him will not perish, but have eternal life. God didn't send his Son into the world to condemn the world, but so the world might be saved through him."

Nicodemus didn't understand all that Jesus was saying, but he became a secret follower.

After the Passover Jesus and his disciples went back to Galilee. On the way they passed through Samaria.

The Jews looked down on the Samaritans and tried not to have anything to do with them. The Samaritans didn't worship God properly, said the Jews. Instead of worshiping at the temple in Jerusalem, they worshiped on their own mountain. The two nations hated each other bitterly.

About noon Jesus and his disciples came to the Samaritan town of Sychar, near the spring called Jacob's Well. Jesus was tired from the journey, so he sat down beside the well. The disciples went into the town to buy supplies.

While Jesus was sitting there, a Samaritan woman came to the well to draw water.

"Give me a drink," Jesus said to her.

"You're a Jew," the woman answered. "How can you ask a Samaritan woman for a drink?"

Jesus answered, "If you only knew who it is that is asking you for a drink, you'd ask him, and he'd give you living water."

"Sir," said the woman, "you don't even have a bucket, and this well is very deep. How can you get this living water? Are you a greater man than

our ancestor, Jacob, who gave us this well and drank from it himself, with his family and his animals?"

Then Jesus told the woman some surprising things. "Whoever drinks this water will be thirsty again," he said. "But whoever drinks the water that I give will never be thirsty again. For the water I give will become a fountain inside, bubbling up into eternal life."

"Sir," said the woman, "give me this water, so I won't be thirsty and have to keep coming to this well."

"Go home and call your husband and then come back here," said Jesus.

"I don't have a husband," she answered.

"You're right to say you don't have a husband," said Jesus. "For you've had five husbands, and the man you're living with now isn't your husband. You spoke the truth then."

"I can see that you're a prophet, sir!" said the woman. "Now, tell me—our ancestors worshiped on this mountain, but you Jews say that Jerusalem is the place we should worship. Who is right? The Samaritans or the Jews?"

"I tell you the truth," said Jesus, "the time is coming when worshiping the Father won't be a question of this mountain or Jerusalem. You Samaritans worship now without understanding, while we Jews understand what we worship, for the salvation of the world will come through the Jews.

"But the time is coming—and is here now—when the real worshipers will worship the Father in Spirit and in truth. Indeed, that's how the Father wants to be worshiped. God is Spirit, and only by the power of the Spirit can people worship him as he really is."

The woman didn't understand what Jesus was saying. "I know the Messiah is coming," she said. "When he comes, he'll make everything clear."

Jesus said, "I who speak to you—I am he."

Just then the disciples arrived. They were surprised to find Jesus having a conversation with a woman. But none of them asked her, "What do you want?" or said to him, "Why are you talking to her?"

The woman put down her water jar and hurried back to the town. She said to the people, "Come and see someone who has told me everything I ever did! Could this be the Messiah?"

The people left the town and started to come to Jesus. Many of the Samaritans who came out of that town believed in him because of what the woman said.

When they arrived, they begged him to stay with them, and he stayed there two days. Many more people had faith because of what he said to them directly.

They told the woman, "Now our faith doesn't depend on what you said, for we've heard him with our own ears. Now we know that he really is the Savior of the world!"

Jesus' New Teaching

Matthew 5—6; Luke 6, 11

JESUS visited Judea, Samaria, and the nearby regions, but he did most of his teaching and healing in the green hills of Galilee. There he told the people the good news of the kingdom of God. Large crowds followed him wherever he went.

One day Jesus went up onto a hillside near Capernaum and sat down. His disciples came to him, and he looked at them and taught them about God's rule, about the kingdom of heaven that was bringing a new way of living into the world.

Blessed are you who are poor,
    for the kingdom of God belongs to you.
Blessed are you who go hungry now,
    for you will be filled.
Blessed are you who weep now,
    for you will laugh.
Blessed are you when people hate you,
    and reject you, and criticize you,
        and say evil things about you for my sake.
Be glad when this happens,
    and jump for joy.
Your reward in heaven will be enormous,
    for that's just the way they treated the
        prophets.
But how terrible for you who are rich;
    you have your comfort now.
How terrible for you who are well-fed,
    for you will go hungry.
How terrible for you who laugh now,
    for you will mourn and weep.
How terrible for you when everyone praises you:
    that's just the way they treated the false
        prophets!

Jesus told his disciples that his teaching was greater than the law of Moses. "But I haven't come to destroy the Law and the Prophets," he said. "I've come to complete them. Not one part of the Scriptures will pass away until every bit of it comes true."

Then he gave them some new teaching. "The old teaching was 'you must not kill,'" he reminded them. "But I tell you, you must not insult anyone. You must not hate anyone.

"The old teaching was 'You must not commit

adultery.' But I tell you, any man who thinks about it, has already committed adultery in his mind.

"You've been taught to pay back exactly what was done to you, to limit your revenge to 'an eye for an eye' and 'a tooth for a tooth.' But I tell you: don't seek revenge. Don't try to get even. If someone slaps you on the cheek, turn and offer the other cheek. If someone takes your shirt, let him have your coat also. If someone forces you to go a mile, do more. Go a second mile also.

"You've been told to love your neighbor and hate your enemy. But I tell you, love your enemies and do good to those who hate you. Bless those who curse you and pray for those who persecute you.

"If you love only those who love you, you're no better than people who don't worship the Lord. Even sinners help those who help them. No. You must be perfect, as your Father in heaven is perfect."

Jesus taught his disciples about helping the poor, about praying, and about fasting. They knew they should do these things, but Jesus warned them to do these things for God, not to impress other people.

"Don't do good deeds in public to attract attention," he said. "If you do, you'll miss the reward your heavenly Father wants to give you.

"When you do good deeds, don't make a big show of it. That's what the hypocrites (the fake

religious people) do. Like play-actors in the synagogues and in the marketplaces, they're hoping that people will admire them. Believe me, they've had all the reward they're going to get!

"Instead, give to the poor in secret. Don't let your left hand know what your right hand is doing. Your Father who sees all secrets will reward you.

"When you pray, don't be like the hypocrites, those play-actors. They love to stand in public places to pray, so everyone will notice them. Believe me, they've had their reward!

"Instead, when you pray, go into a room by

yourself, shut the door, and pray to your Father in secret. Your Father who sees all secrets will reward you.

"When you pray, don't babble like the pagans. People who don't know God think they'll be heard because they use a lot of words. Don't be like them. Your heavenly Father knows what you need before you ask.

"When you pray, pray like this:

Our Father in heaven,
    holy is your name!

May your kingdom come;
may your will be done
    on earth as it is in heaven.

Give us each day the food we need,
and forgive us the wrong we have done,
    as we forgive those who have wronged us.

Don't bring us to the test,
    but save us from the evil one.

"And when you fast," said Jesus, "don't look gloomy, like the hypocrites. They try to let everyone see how hungry they are. Believe me, they've had their reward!

"Instead, when you fast, wash your face and comb your hair, so no one can tell that you're fasting—no one except your heavenly Father. Your Father who sees all secrets will reward you."

15

Trusting God

Matthew 6—7; Luke 6, 11—12

PUT God first," Jesus taught his disciples. "Everything else depends on that.

"Don't pile up treasures for yourself on earth, where moths and rust can spoil them and robbers can break in and steal them.

"Instead, keep your treasures in heaven, where moths and rust can't destroy them, and robbers can't break in and steal them. Remember. Wherever your treasure is, that's where your heart will be.

"No one can be loyal to two masters. You can't

serve God and money. So I tell you, don't worry about your life, what you'll eat and drink, or about your body and what you'll wear. Certainly your life means more than food, and your body means more than clothing.

"Look at the birds in the sky. They don't plant or harvest or store their food. Yet your heavenly Father feeds them. And you're certainly worth more than birds!

"With all your worrying, can any of you add a moment to the length of your life? Well, if the smallest things are beyond your power, why worry about the rest?

"Look at the lilies in the field. They don't spin thread or weave cloth. I tell you, not even King Solomon in all his glory was as well-dressed as one of those flowers! If that's how God takes care of wild flowers, which are here today and gone tomorrow, won't he take care of you? O people, what little faith you have!

"Stop worrying. Stop asking, 'What will we eat; what will we drink; what will we wear?' These are questions for people who don't know God. Let the pagans worry about such things, not you. Your heavenly Father knows that you need all these things.

"Instead, put your mind on God's rule, and think about his righteousness. Then all these other things will be given to you."

Jesus wanted his disciples to trust God completely and to treat other people kindly.

"Always treat other people as you want them to treat you," he said. "That's the meaning of all the Scriptures, the whole Law and the Prophets.

"Don't judge other people, and God won't judge you. Forgive other people, and God will forgive you. Give, and God will give gifts to you.

"Why do you stare at the speck in your brother's eye and pay no attention to the log in your own eye? How can you say to your brother, 'Brother, let me take that speck out of your eye,' when you don't see the log in your own eye? You hypocrite! First take the log out of your own eye. Then you'll see well enough to take the speck out of your brother's eye."

Trusting God can be hard. Following Jesus' teaching is difficult. But any other way of living leads to disaster, Jesus said.

"Some people call me Lord and never do what I tell them," he said. "Whoever comes to me and listens to my teaching and obeys—I'll tell you what that person's like. He's like a wise man building a house. The wise man dug deep and laid the foundation on rock. When the flood came, the water rushed against the side of that house, but it didn't fall, because it was built on the rock.

"Whoever hears my teaching and doesn't obey is like a foolish man building a house. The foolish man built his house on sand, with no foundation. When the flood came, the house collapsed. And what a great disaster it was!"

Then he said to them, "Would any of you fathers give your son a stone if he asked you for bread? Or would you hand him a snake if he asked for a fish? If you sinners know how to give good gifts to your children, how much more will your heavenly Father give good things to those who ask him!"

16

Jesus Does
the Works of God

Matthew 8, 11; Luke 7; John 4

A ROMAN army officer had a servant he cared about very much. The servant was seriously ill. When the officer heard about Jesus, he went to Jesus and said, "Sir, my servant is in bed, paralyzed and in pain."

"I'll come and heal him," said Jesus.

"Don't go to any trouble, sir," said the officer. "I'm not worthy for you to come to my house. Instead, just give the order from here, and my servant will be healed. I'm an army officer; I understand giving and taking orders."

Jesus was amazed at the faith of this pagan Roman. "I tell you the truth," he said to the crowd following him, "I haven't found faith like this anywhere in Israel."

Then he said to the officer, "Go home now. Everything will be as you have believed."

When the officer arrived home, he found that his servant had been healed at exactly the hour Jesus had spoken.

Right after this, Jesus went to a town called Nain. His disciples went with him, and so did a great crowd of people. As he came near the gate of the town, he saw a funeral procession coming out. They were carrying the body of a man who was the only son of a widow. A large number of people from the town were with her.

When Jesus saw her, he had pity on her. "Don't cry any more," he said. Then he walked over and touched her son's coffin.

The men carrying the coffin stopped.

"Rise up, young man!" said Jesus.

The man sat up and began to speak, and Jesus gave him back to his mother.

The people were filled with wonder, and they began to praise God. "A great prophet has appeared among us," they said. "God has visited his people!"

The news of these great works spread everywhere, even to the prison where Herod Antipas, ruler of Galilee, had locked up John the Baptist. John had become discouraged in prison and he

began to doubt Jesus. He sent two of his disciples to go to Jesus with a question.

When John's disciples came to Jesus, they saw the miracles he was working. Then they asked him John's question.

"Are you the one who is to come," they said, "or should we look for someone else?"

Jesus answered, "Go back and tell John what you have seen and heard. The blind can see again. The lame can walk. Lepers are made clean. The deaf can hear. And the poor hear the good news."

Then he added, "Blessed is the person who doesn't lose faith in me."

After John's disciples left, Jesus turned to the crowd and spoke to them about John.

"When you went out into the wilderness," he said, "What did you expect to see? A straw blowing in the wind? Of course not.

"What did you go out there for? To see a man

dressed in fine clothes? Well, you have to go to a palace to see people wearing fine clothes and living in luxury.

"What did you really go out there for? To see a prophet? I tell you, you saw something greater than a prophet! John is the one that Scripture describes:

Here is my messenger, whom I send ahead of you;
    he will prepare the way before you.

"I tell you the truth, no human has ever lived who is greater than John. Yet, the least important person in the kingdom of God is greater than John. For John is the one who was chosen by God to come before the kingdom, to prepare the way.

"The people who listened to John's preaching understood what God wanted them to do. They turned from their sins and let John baptize them. But the Pharisees refused to be baptized. When they refused John's baptism, they refused God's salvation."

Then Jesus said, "How can I describe the people of today? They're like children sitting in the market place. One group shouts to another:

We played wedding music for you,
    but you wouldn't dance.
We played funeral songs,
    but you wouldn't cry.

"John came, living according to strict rules, and people said, 'He's crazy!' Then the Son of Man came, enjoying himself, and they said, 'Look at him. He eats and drinks too much. He's a friend of tax collectors and sinners!'

"But God's works prove his wisdom," said Jesus.

17

"What Is the Kingdom of God Like?"

Matthew 9, 12—13; Mark 3—4; Luke 8, 11, 13

JESUS must be crazy!" said some people.

"He's possessed by a demon," said the Pharisees. "He drives out demons, sure, but he does it by the power of Beelzebul, the prince of demons."

Jesus knew what they were thinking. "You say I'm crazy," he answered, "but how could one demon drive out another? Can Satan drive out Satan? If he fights with himself, his kingdom can't stand. A kingdom that's divided against itself will fall down.

"But if I drive out demons by the power of God,

then the kingdom of God is already here!"

This talk about Jesus being crazy, being possessed by a demon, reached his family. They began to worry about him. Finally, they came to get him and take him home. But the crowd around the house where he was staying was so large, they couldn't get inside.

"Your mother and your brothers are standing outside," they told Jesus. "They want to see you."

"Who is my mother?" asked Jesus. "Who are my brothers?"

He looked at the disciples sitting around him. "See!" he said. "Here are my mother and my brothers. Whoever hears the word of God and does it—that person is my brother, my sister, my mother!"

Jesus was saying these things to show his disciples what the kingdom of God is like. Another way he taught about the kingdom was by telling simple stories called parables.

Jesus left the house and went to the shore of the Sea of Galilee. A huge crowd gathered around him, trying to touch him. There were so many people, he got into a boat and sat in it, out in the water, while the people listened from the shore. They crowded all the way to the edge of the water.

Then Jesus spoke to them in parables so they would think about what the kingdom of God was like.

"Once a farmer went out to plant some seed,"

he said. "As he sowed the seed, some of it fell beside the path, and the birds came and ate it up.

"Some seeds fell on stony ground, where there wasn't much soil. The seed sprouted and grew quickly in that shallow soil. Then the sun came up and burned the little plants and they dried up because they had no roots.

"Some seeds fell among thorn bushes, and when the throns grew up they choked the plants.

"But other seeds fell into good soil. When the plants sprouted they produced a crop of grain—a hundred seeds of grain for each seed that was planted."

Then Jesus said to the people, "Listen, everyone who has ears to hear!"

Later, when he was alone with his disciples, they asked him, "Why do you speak to them in parables?"

Jesus answered, "The secrets of the kingdom of God have been given to you, but the others don't understand. It's what the prophet Isaiah said:

> They look and don't see;
> > they listen and don't understand.

> Their minds are closed;
> > their ears and eyes are dull.

> If they would look and listen,
> > they would understand;

> If they understood,
> > they would turn to God and be saved!"

Then Jesus explained to his disciples what the parable meant.

"The farmer is planting the message about the kingdom of God," he said. "Whoever hears without understanding is like the seed that fell beside the path. Satan comes and snatches it away.

"The seed planted on stony ground is like the people who hear the message and accept it with joy right away. But it doesn't put down roots, so it doesn't last. As soon as something comes and gives them trouble because of the message, they dry up and lose their faith.

"The seed that fell among thorns is like the people who hear the message but don't produce anything, because they're choked by the problems and pleasures of life. They don't produce anything; their fruit doesn't ripen.

"But the seed that fell into good soil is like the people who listen to the message and understand. Their lives produce a great crop, a hundred times as much as was planted."

Jesus told the people many other parables about the kingdom, and later, when he was alone with his disciples, he explained them.

"What is the kingdom of God like?" he asked. "It's like a mustard seed which a man took and planted in his garden. It grew and became a tree, and the birds of the air built their nests in its branches.

"What else is the kingdom of God like? It's like the yeast which a woman took and mixed with three measures of flour. It made the whole batch of dough rise.

"The kingdom of God is like a treasure hidden in a field. A man discovers it, buries it again, and goes off and sells everything he has so he can buy the field.

"And the kingdom of God is like a merchant looking for fine pearls. When he finds a valuable one, he goes and sells everything he owns and buys it.

"That's what the kingdom of God is like."

18

"Who Is This Man?"

Matthew 8; Mark 4—5; Luke 8

JESUS spent the whole day teaching the people about the kingdom of God. In the evening he said to his disciples, "Let's cross over to the other side of the lake."

They pushed off from the shore in the little boat he had been sitting in, leaving the crowd behind them. As they sailed along, Jesus fell asleep.

Suddenly a great storm blew across the lake, and a strong wind pushed water into the boat. They were in real danger of sinking.

The disciples went to Jesus, who was in the

back of the boat, asleep with his head on a pillow.

"Teacher, teacher!" they cried. "We're sinking fast! Don't you care?"

Jesus stood up and gave an order to the wind and the water.

"Be quiet!" he commanded the wind. "Be still!" he ordered the waves.

The wind quieted down, and the sea became completely still.

"Why are you so frightened?" he asked the disciples. "Don't you have any faith?"

They were filled with wonder. "Who is this man?" they asked each other. "Even the wind and the sea obey him!"

Then they arrived at the other side of the lake, in the land of the Gerasenes, near the Greek city of Gadara.

As soon as Jesus stepped ashore, he was met by a man who was a maniac. This man had been suffering a long time from demons seizing him. They made him behave so violently that nobody could control him. He would snap the chains that were put on him, and the demons would drive him away into deserted places. There he wandered naked among the tombs and through the hills, howling and slashing himself with stones.

Now, as soon as he saw Jesus, the man ran and threw himself down at his feet.

"Come out of this man, you unclean spirit!" ordered Jesus.

The man screamed at the top of his voice,

"What do you want with me, Jesus, Son of God the Most High? I beg you, don't torture me!"

"What is your name?" asked Jesus.

"My name is Legion," answered the man, "because there's a whole army of evil spirits in me!" And he begged Jesus not to order the spirits into the depths of the earth.

A large herd of pigs happened to be grazing on a hillside nearby, and the demons said, "Send us into the pigs!"

"Go!" Jesus commanded.

The demons left the man and went into the pigs. Then the whole herd of pigs, thousands of them, stampeded over the edge of the cliff and into the lake, where they drowned.

When the men who had been taking care of the pigs saw what had happened, they ran into the town and told everyone about it.

The people of the town came out to see for themselves. When they came near Jesus, they were shocked to find the maniac sitting there, wearing clothes and in his right mind. They were filled with fear.

Everyone in the land of the Gerasenes heard what had happened, and they were so upset they begged Jesus to leave the neighborhood.

As Jesus was stepping into the boat to go back across the lake, the man who had been healed begged him, "Let me go with you."

But Jesus sent the man away. "Go back home now," he said, "and tell your people everything that God has done for you."

The man went back to town, telling everyone what Jesus had done for him.

19

Jesus Heals a Woman and a Little Girl

Matthew 9; Mark 5; Luke 8

BACK on the other side of the lake, a huge crowd was waiting for Jesus. When he returned, a man named Jairus, a leader of the synagogue, came and fell at his feet.

"My little daughter is very sick," said Jairus. "She's dying. I beg you, come and lay your hands on her, and she will be healed!" She was his only daughter, just twelve years old.

Jesus went with him, and the crowd followed behind. The people were pushing against him on every side.

In the crowd was a woman who had been suffering from severe bleeding for twelve years. She had spent all her money on doctors, but no one could help her.

As she pushed through the crowd behind Jesus, she was saying to herself, "If I can just touch his clothes, I'll be cured."

As soon as she touched the edge of his robe, her bleeding stopped. She could feel that she was healed.

At the same time, Jesus turned around and asked, "Who touched me?"

Everyone said they didn't do it.

"Teacher," said Simon Peter, "the crowd is pressing so close against you, how could you ask who touched you?"

"Someone touched me," said Jesus. "I could feel power going out of me."

Then the woman stepped forward, trembling with fear. She fell at his feet. Right there in front of everyone she told Jesus why she had touched him and how she had been healed.

"My daughter," said Jesus, "your faith has brought you salvation. Go in peace."

While he was still speaking, a messenger arrived from Jairus' house. "Your daughter has just died," he said to Jairus. "Don't bother the teacher any more."

When Jesus heard what the messenger said, he turned to Jairus. "Don't be afraid," he said. "Just have faith, and she will live!"

They went on to Jairus' house. When Jesus arrived, he found a noisy crowd of musicians and mourners in the house. People were already gathering for the funeral.

"Why all this confusion?" Jesus said when they went in. "Why are you crying? The child isn't dead. She's sleeping."

They laughed at him, but Jesus sent them outside.

Then he took the child's parents and Simon Peter, John, and James, and went into the room where the girl was lying. He went up to her and took her by the hand.

"Talitha kum," he said, (which means, "Little girl, I tell you, get up!").

Her breath came back and she stood up and

started walking around. Jesus told them to give her something to eat.

Her parents were amazed. Jesus told them not to tell anyone what had happened, but the news spread all over the countryside.

20

Power to Defeat the Enemy

Matthew 10, 14; Mark 3, 6; Luke 6, 9—10, 12; John 4

JESUS kept on traveling through the towns and villages of Galilee, teaching the people about the kingdom of God and healing them of their diseases. As he looked at the crowds, he felt pity for them, because they were as helpless as sheep without a shepherd.

"See them," he said to his disciples. "They're like a great field of wheat, ripe and ready to harvest. But there aren't many workers. Pray for the Lord of the harvest to send out workers to gather this harvest!"

He was talking about the harvest of people that God wanted to gather for eternal life.

Then Jesus went out into the hills by himself, where he spent the whole night praying to the Lord.

The next morning he called his disciples to him and chose some of them to send out as missionaries. These men were called apostles, which means "sent." The twelve leaders were—

Simon, whom Jesus called Peter, and his brother, Andrew.

James and John, the sons of Zebedee, whom Jesus called "the sons of thunder."

Philip.

Bartholomew.

Thomas.

Matthew, also called Levi, a tax collector.

James, the son of Alpheus.

Thaddeus.

Simon the Zealot, a member of a rebel anti-Roman group.

And Judas Iscariot, who later betrayed Jesus.

Jesus said to them, "I have chosen you. I'm going to send you out to preach the good news that the kingdom of God is here."

He sent them ahead of him, two by two, to every town and place that he planned to visit. He gave them power to drive out demons and to heal the sick.

Before these missionaries left, Jesus gave them some instructions. "Don't take anything with you for the journey," he said. "No money, no knapsack, no extra clothes. Stay wherever you're welcomed. If you're not welcomed in one town, leave it and go to another. Shake the dust from your feet as you leave. Whoever welcomes you welcomes me, and whoever welcomes me welcomes the one who sent me.

"I'm sending you out like sheep among wolves. Be as smart as snakes but as harmless as doves. Don't be afraid. God will take care of you."

Sometime later the missionaries returned, full of joy because they had preached the good news and healed many sick people.

"Teacher," they said, "even the demons obeyed

us when we commanded them in your name!"

When he heard this report, Jesus told them about a vision he had seen.

"I watched Satan fall like lightning from heaven!" he said. "See, I've given you the power to defeat the enemy. Nothing will harm you. But don't be glad that spirits obey you. Instead, be glad that your names are written in heaven!"

At that moment Jesus was filled with joy by the Holy Spirit and he said, "I praise you, Father, Lord of heaven and earth! You have hidden these things from the wise and educated people, and you have shown them to ordinary people."

Then he turned to the apostles and said, "Blessed are the eyes that see what you see. I tell you, many prophets and kings have wanted to see what you see and haven't seen it, to hear what you hear, and haven't heard it!"

Even at this time of victory over evil, the power of evil was still at work.

Herod Antipas had arrested John the Baptist and had him chained in prison. Herod was upset because John had criticized him for marrying Herodias, his brother's wife. Herodias was so angry, she wanted to kill John, but she couldn't, because Herod was afraid of John. He knew that John was a holy man respected by the people. He used to listen to John himself. Even though John's preaching bothered him, he still enjoyed hearing him.

On Herod's birthday Herodias found her

chance. Herod gave a party for his officials and the important people of Galilee. Herodias' daughter came in and danced, delighting Herod and his guests.

Herod was so pleased with her, he said, "Ask me for anything. I'll give you whatever you want, even half my kingdom!"

The girl went out and asked her mother, "What should I say?"

Herodias answered, "Ask for the head of John the Baptist, on a plate!"

The girl rushed back to Herod and said, "I want you to give me, right now, the head of John the Baptist on a plate!"

Herod was horrified. But he had made a promise in front of his guests, so he didn't refuse her. He immediately sent a guard with orders to bring John's head back to the palace.

The guard went to the prison and cut off John's head and brought it back to the palace, on a plate. He gave it to the girl, who took it to her mother.

When John's disciples heard what had happened, they came and took the body and buried it. Then they went and told Jesus.

Jesus was so upset by what had happened to his friend and cousin, he went off by himself in a boat, to be alone in a deserted place. This happened right after the missionaries returned.

Who Do You
Say That I Am?

21

Bread from Heaven

Matthew 14; Mark 6; Luke 9; John 6

WHEN the crowds heard that Jesus had gone off by himself, they came out from all the towns and ran ahead of him on land. When he saw them, he felt pity for them and began to teach them and heal them.

Late in the afternoon the disciples came to Jesus and said, "It's late, and this is a deserted place. Send the people to the villages near here so they can buy some food."

"Don't send them away," said Jesus. "Feed them yourselves."

"What?" asked Philip. "Do you expect us to go out and buy food? Even if we spent two hundred pieces of silver, we couldn't buy any more than a bite for each person!"

"How much food do you have?" asked Jesus. "Go and find out."

They did as he said, and Andrew came back to report. "There's a little boy here who has five loaves of barley bread and a couple of dried fish," he said. "But what good could that be for so many?"

"Bring them here to me," said Jesus.

Then he told the disciples to divide the people into groups and have them sit down on the green grass in a hundred rows of fifty each. They did, and the people sat down.

Jesus took the loaves and fishes, looked up to heaven, and thanked God for them. Then he broke the food into pieces and gave it to his disciples to pass out among the people.

Five thousand people, not counting the women and children, ate their fill.

When they had all they wanted, Jesus said to his disciples, "Collect the food that is left over. Don't let anything be wasted."

They gathered twelve basketsful of bread and fish.

When the people realized what Jesus had done, they said, "This is really the one who is to come into the world!"

Jesus realized that they were going to come

and carry him off by force to make him king, so he escaped to the hills by himself to pray.

That evening the disciples went down to the shore of the lake and got into a boat to cross back to Capernaum. The boat went far out onto the lake. Evening came and it was dark. A strong wind began to blow and the sea became rough.

The disciples rowed about three or four miles. Then they saw Jesus coming toward the boat. He was walking on the water.

"It's a ghost!" they thought, and they screamed with terror.

Immediately Jesus said to them, "Be brave. It is I. Don't be afraid."

"Lord," said Simon Peter, "if it's really you, order me to come to you on the water."

"Come," said Jesus.

Simon got out of the boat and started walking on the water toward Jesus. But as soon as he felt the strong wind, he was afraid, and he began to sink.

"Lord, save me!" he cried.

Jesus immediately reached out and caught him. "O man of little faith," he said. "Why did you doubt?"

They climbed into the boat, and the wind stopped blowing.

The disciples were filled with wonder. They bowed down before him and said, "Truly, you are the Son of God!"

Then the boat reached the shore, and the next morning the people crossed the lake looking for him. "Teacher," they said when they found him, "when did you get here?"

"I tell you the truth," he answered, "you're looking for me because you were fed, but not because you understand the meaning of the loaves and fishes."

Then he said to them, "Don't work for food that doesn't last. Work for the bread the Son of Man will give you, the bread that lasts for eternal life."

"What do we have to do?" the people asked.

Jesus answered, "This is what God wants you to do: have faith in the one he has sent."

Then the people said, "What will you do to prove we can trust you? God sent our ancestors bread from heaven when they were in the wilderness."

Jesus answered, "Your ancestors died. The real

bread of God comes down from heaven and gives life to the world."

"Sir," they begged, "give us this bread all the time."

"I am the bread of life," Jesus answered. "Whoever comes to me will never be hungry. Whoever believes in me will have eternal life."

"What?" said the people. "How can he say he came down from heaven? This is Jesus, the son of Joseph. We know his father!"

"I am the bread of life," said Jesus. "Whoever eats this bread will never die. The bread I give is my body, for the life of the world."

The people didn't like what Jesus was saying. "How can he give us his body to eat?" they complained to each other.

"I tell you the truth," said Jesus, "if you don't eat the body of the Son of Man, and drink his blood, you won't have life. Just as the living Father sent me, and I have life through him, whoever feeds on me will have life through me."

"These are difficult sayings," complained the people. "Who can accept this?"

Jesus knew what they were thinking. "Does this ruin your faith?" he asked. "The words I have spoken are spirit and life, but you don't believe. No one can come to me unless the Father makes it possible."

After this many of Jesus' followers left him and turned back. They refused to go with him anymore

"Do you want to leave, too?" he said to the twelve apostles.

Simon Peter answered, "Lord, who else could we follow? You have the words of eternal life. We have faith in you. We're sure that you're the Holy One of God!"

22

Pharisees and Foreigners

Matthew 15; Mark 7—8; Luke 8

SOME scribes and Pharisees came from Jerusalem to Galilee to spy on Jesus. They listened to his teaching and watched how he acted with his disciples.

They noticed that some of his disciples ate without first washing their hands. The Pharisees never ate without washing themselves in a special way. They followed many rules about clean and unclear food and washing cups and plates and bowls. They were sure that their rules made them pure in the eyes of God.

"Why don't your disciples do things our way?" they asked Jesus. "Why do they eat without washing their hands properly?"

"You Pharisees!" said Jesus. "You clean the outside of your plates and cups, but inside you're filthy with greed and wickedness. You give God a tenth of all your garden herbs, but you ignore justice. You carefully follow your own rules, but you think nothing of breaking God's laws!

"The prophet Isaiah meant you people when he said:

These people honor God with their lips,
but their hearts are far from him.

Their worship means nothing,
because they teach human rules
as if they were the laws of God!"

Then Jesus turned to the crowd and said, "Listen to me, all of you: nothing that goes into a person from the outside can make one unclean in the eyes of God. It's what comes out of a person that makes one unclean."

Later, when Jesus left the crowd and went into the house where he was staying, his disciples came to him and said, "The Pharisees were offended by what you said."

"Ignore them," he answered. "They're blind guides. When one blind person tries to lead someone else, they both fall into the ditch!"

"Tell us what you meant," said Simon.

"Don't you understand yet?" said Jesus. "Don't you see that eating certain foods can't make a person unclean? It's what comes out of your mouth that makes you unclean.

"Whatever goes into your mouth passes through your stomach and out of your body. But what comes out of your mouth is from the mind: evil thoughts of murder, adultery, lying, cheating, stealing, jealousy, gossip, and pride. Those are the things that make a person unclean, not eating without washing your hands!"

While the scribes and Pharisees were criticizing Jesus, the sinners and foreigners that they didn't like were accepting him, and many women were following him. Mary Magdalene, Joanna, Susanna, and other women traveled with Jesus and his disciples, providing for them with their own money. Jesus had healed them of evil spirits and diseases, and they believed in him.

When Jesus went outside of Galilee and into the Syrian countryside near Tyre, a Syrian woman came to him and asked for help. "Have pity on me," she cried. "My daughter is being tortured by a demon!"

She fell at his feet, but Jesus didn't say anything to her.

"Send her away," said the disciples. "She's been following us and shouting." They knew he wanted to be alone, to rest from the crowds.

"Help me," begged the woman again.

Jesus looked at her and said, "I've been sent to the lost sheep of Israel, not to foreign nations. It's not right to take the children's food and throw it to the dogs."

"Ah, yes," the woman answered. "But even the dogs eat the crumbs that fall from their master's table."

"What an answer!" said Jesus. "With faith like that, you may go home happy, for the demon has left your daughter."

She went home and found her child completely cured, just as Jesus had said.

Other foreigners had faith in Jesus. As he traveled, he passed through some cities where many Greeks lived. Crowds came to him with their sick friends and relatives, and he healed them.

He touched a man who couldn't hear or speak, and the man was cured. They brought him a blind man, and he opened the man's eyes.

The Greeks were amazed. "Everything he does, he does well," they said. "He makes the deaf hear and the dumb speak and the blind see!"

These foreigners had more faith than the Pharisees. They didn't know the Scriptures. They hadn't been taught the Law and the Prophets. But they believed that Jesus could heal them.

The Pharisees kept watching Jesus. But even though they saw him work miracles, they still didn't believe in him. Instead of turning to Jesus, they plotted against him. No matter what he said and did, they paid no attention.

23

"Who Do You Say That I Am?"

Matthew 16—17; Mark 8—9; Luke 9, 12

T ELL me," Jesus asked his disciples. "Who do people say that I am?" They were traveling north of Galilee into the region of Iturea, walking from village to village. Now they were coming near the city of Caesarea Philippi.

The disciples answered, "Some say you're John the Baptist. Others say you're Elijah. And some say you're Jeremiah or one of the other prophets come back to life."

"What about you?" asked Jesus. "Who do you say that I am?"

113

Simon answered, "You are the Messiah, the Son of the living God!"

"Blessed are you, Simon!" said Jesus. "This wasn't shown to you by man, but by my heavenly Father.

"Now, I tell you, your name will be Peter, 'the rock.' On this rock I will build my church, and the powers of hell will never defeat it. I'll give you the keys of the kingdom. Whatever you forbid on earth will be what is forbidden in heaven. Whatever you allow on earth will be what is allowed in heaven."

Then he added, "Don't tell anyone about this yet."

After this conversation, Jesus began to teach his disciples about his death. "The Son of Man must suffer many things," he told them. "He must go to Jerusalem and be rejected by the elders, the chief priests, and the scribes. He'll be put to death, and he'll be raised from the dead on the third day."

Peter took Jesus by the arm and began to argue with him. "Heaven forbid, Lord!" he said. "This must not happen to you."

Jesus turned and said to Peter, "Get out of my way, you Satan! You're a stumbling block to me. Those are human thoughts, not God's thoughts."

Then he said to the disciples, "If you're going to follow me, you must not think about yourself. You must be ready to suffer. That's the way to have real life."

114

Six days later Jesus took Peter and James and John and led them up a high mountain, where they were alone. While Jesus prayed, the three disciples saw his appearance change right in front of them. His face suddenly began to shine like the sun, and his clothes became dazzling, unearthly white.

They saw Moses and Elijah standing beside Jesus, talking about how he would go to Jerusalem and suffer.

Then the vision of Moses and Elijah began to fade, and Peter blurted out, "Teacher, how wonderful it is for us to be here! Let us make three

shelters—one for you, one for Moses, and one for Elijah."

He didn't know what he was talking about.

While Peter was still speaking, a bright cloud appeared. The shadow of the cloud passed over the disciples, and they felt afraid.

From the cloud came a voice, saying, "This is my beloved Son. Listen to him."

When they heard the voice, the three disciples fell on their faces, full of fear.

Jesus went to them and touched them. "Stand up," he said. "Don't be afraid."

They looked up. No one was there except Jesus.

On the way down from the mountain Jesus warned them, "Don't tell anyone what you've seen until after the Son of Man rises from the dead."

"What does 'rising from the dead' mean?" they asked each other. They couldn't figure it out.

Then they asked Jesus, "Why do the scribes say that Elijah must return before the Messiah comes?"

"That's right," he answered. "Elijah comes first, to prepare everything. I tell you, Elijah has already been here, but they didn't recognize him. They treated him as they pleased."

The disciples understood that he was talking about John the Baptist.

Then Jesus said, "They'll do the same to the Son of Man as they did to John, because Scripture says the Son of Man must suffer."

116

Hard Lessons for the Disciples

Matthew 17—18; Mark 9; Luke 9, 17

WHEN Jesus and Peter, James, and John came down from the mountain, they returned to the place where they had left the other disciples. They found a huge crowd around the disciples and some scribes arguing with them.

As soon as they saw Jesus, the disciples ran up to him and welcomed him. "What are you arguing about with the scribes?" he asked.

"Teacher," said a man in the crowd, "I brought my son to you—my only child. He has an evil spirit in him. It attacks him and throws him to

117

the ground, and he foams at the mouth and grinds his teeth and doesn't move. I asked your disciples to drive the demon out, but they couldn't."

Jesus looked at the disciples and said, "O what unbelieving people you are! How much longer must I be with you? How long do I have to put up with you?"

Then he said to the man, "Bring the boy to me."

They brought the boy to him, and as soon as the demon saw Jesus, it threw the boy into a fit. He fell to the ground and rolled around, foaming at the mouth.

"How long has this been going on?" Jesus asked the father.

"Ever since he was a child. It has often tried to

kill him by throwing him into the fire or the water. If it's possible, please have pity on us and help us."

"If it's possible?" said Jesus. "Everything's possible for someone who has faith!"

"I have faith!" cried the boy's father. "Help me have more faith."

Then Jesus said to the evil spirit, "Deaf and dumb spirit, I command you: come out of this boy and never go into him again!"

The demon screamed and threw the boy into a violent fit. Then it went out of him. He lay on the ground like a corpse.

"He's dead," said the people in the crowd.

But Jesus took the boy by the hand and lifted him to his feet, and the boy stood up.

Later, when Jesus and his disciples went indoors, they asked him, "Why couldn't we drive out the demon?"

"Because you have so little faith," he answered.

"Increase our faith!" they said.

"If you had faith the size of a tiny mustard seed," he said, "you could tell this mountain to move, and it would move. Nothing would be impossible.

"I tell you the truth. Whenever two of you on earth agree about anything in prayer, it will be done for you by my Father in heaven. Whenever two or three persons meet together in my name, I will be with them."

This teaching on faith was difficult for the disciples. Even though they were close to Jesus and saw the great works he did, they still had trouble believing in him.

They also had trouble understanding what he was saying about his death. As they walked back to Capernaum, he spoke to them again about his suffering.

"The Son of Man must be handed over to the power of men," he said. "They will put him to death, and on the third day he will rise again."

They didn't understand, but they were afraid to ask him what he meant. They had another problem. When they arrived back in Capernaum, and went indoors, Jesus spoke to them about it.

"What were you arguing about on the way?" he asked.

They didn't answer, because they had been arguing about which of them was the greatest.

Jesus knew what was on their minds, so he sat down and called the twelve men to him. "Whoever wants to be first must put himself last," he said. "You must be the servant of others."

Then Jesus took a little child and stood the child in front of them. He put his arms around the child and said, "I tell you the truth. Unless you change and become like little children, you won't enter the kingdom of God. Whoever humbles oneself like a child is the greatest in the kingdom.

Rivers of Living Water

John 7—8

JESUS went to Jerusalem for the fall harvest festival, the feast of Succoth, even though he knew it was dangerous. The religious leaders in Jerusalem were looking for an excuse to get rid of him.

At the feast they were looking for him. "Where is that man?" they asked.

People stood around in groups, whispering about him. "He's a good man," said some.

"No," said others. "He lies to the people."

No one would speak about him publicly, be-

cause they were afraid of the leaders—the elders, the chief priests, and the scribes.

When the feast was half over, Jesus went into the temple area and began to teach. The religious leaders were surprised when they heard him.

"How did this fellow get his education?" they asked. "He has had no teacher."

Jesus answered, "My teaching comes from the one who sent me. You say you obey the law of Moses, but you don't follow his teaching. Why are you looking for an excuse to kill me?"

"You're crazy!" they said. "Who wants to kill you?"

Although these powerful men hated Jesus, many of the common people believed in him.

They kept saying, "When the Messiah comes, could he give more signs or work more miracles than this man?"

The Pharisees were furious when they heard such things, and they sent the temple police to arrest him.

On the last and greatest day of the feast, when the people were praying for rain, Jesus stood up and cried out, "If anyone is thirsty, come to me. Let whoever believes in me drink. For Scripture says whoever has faith in me will have

> rivers of living water
> flowing from within him."

Jesus was talking about the Holy Spirit, which he later gave to his church.

"Surely, he must be a prophet," said the people who heard him.

"This is the Messiah!" said other people.

"No," said some others. "The Messiah can't come from Galilee. Doesn't Scripture say that the Messiah must be from the family of David, from the town of Bethlehem?" They were sure that Jesus came from Nazareth.

They couldn't agree. Some wanted to arrest him, but no one touched him. Finally, the temple police returned empty-handed to the chief priests and the Pharisees.

"Why didn't you bring Jesus?" they asked.

The police answered, "There's never been

anyone who speaks as he does."

"Aha!" said the Pharisees. "He's fooled you, too. Now, listen. Have any of the leaders believed in him? Have the members of the council believed in him? The Pharisees? No! It's just this mob, these ignorant people. And they're doomed anyway!"

Nicodemus, the Pharisee who had gone to Jesus one night during Passover, now spoke up. "Since when does our law condemn a man without first hearing him and finding out the facts?" he said.

"Well!" they sneered. "Don't tell us you're a Galilean, too! Look it up in the Scriptures and see for yourself. The Messiah couldn't possibly come from Galilee!"

The Light of the World

John 8—10

DURING the last part of the feast, when the lights were being lit, Jesus said to the people, "I am the light of the world. Whoever follows me will never walk in darkness. If you believe my message, you will know the truth, and the truth will set you free."

When he said this, the religious leaders became so angry, they called him a Samaritan. They said he was crazy. They said he was possessed by a demon. They accused him of insulting God, which was the crime of blasphemy.

Then they picked up stones to throw at him, trying to kill him, but he slipped away.

This same day, as Jesus was walking in Jerusalem with his disciples, he saw a man who had been born blind.

"Teacher," said the disciples, "who committed the sin that caused him to be born blind—this man or his parents?"

They had been taught that disease was a punishment, so Jesus' answer surprised them.

"Neither," he said. "This man wasn't born blind because of his sin nor the sin of his parents. He was born blind to show the power of God at work."

Then he explained, "While I am in the world, I

am the light of the world," and he worked a miracle to show the power of God. He spit on the ground and made a paste and smeared it over the blind man's eyes. Then he told the man, "Go and wash in the Pool of Siloam."

The blind man went away and washed himself. Then he returned—able to see.

His neighbors and the people who were used to seeing him began to ask each other, "Isn't this the fellow who used to sit and beg?"

"Yes," said some of them. "It's the very same man."

"No," said others. "It's just someone who looks like him."

The man himself said, "I am the one."

So they said to him, "How were your eyes opened?"

He answered, "The man they call Jesus made a paste and smeared it on my eyes and told me to go and wash at Siloam. When I went and washed, I could see."

"Where is he?" they asked, meaning Jesus.

"I don't know," he answered.

They took the man who had been blind to the Pharisees. It was a Sabbath day when Jesus made the paste and opened the man's eyes. The Pharisees asked him how he had been healed, and he said, "He put a paste on my eyes, and I washed, and now I can see."

Some of the Pharisees said, "This man isn't from God. He doesn't keep the Sabbath."

Others said, "How could anyone do such miracles and be a sinner?"

They couldn't agree, so they spoke to the blind man again. "Since he has opened your eyes," they asked, "what do you have to say about him?"

"He's a prophet," he answered.

The Pharisees refused to believe that he had really been blind and had been healed, so they sent for his parents. "Is this man your son?" they asked. "Was he born blind? If so, how can he now see?"

His parents answered, "We know that this is our son and that he was born blind. But we don't know how he can see now or who opened his eyes. He's old enough. Let him speak for himself."

They answered like this because they were afraid. The religious leaders had already agreed that anyone who believed that Jesus was the Messiah would be thrown out of the synagogue. That was why his parents told them to ask the man himself.

So they called the man back a second time and said to him, "Give glory to God—admit that this man is a sinner!"

The man answered, "I don't know whether or not he's a sinner. One thing I do know—I was blind and now I can see."

"What did he do to you?" they asked. "How did he open your eyes?"

"I've told you once, and you didn't pay attention. Why do you want to hear it all over again?

Do you want to become his disciples, too?"

The Pharisees were annoyed at this answer, and they insulted him. "You can be his disciple," they said. "We're disciples of Moses. We know that God spoke to Moses, but we don't even know where this fellow comes from."

"Now that's strange," said the man. "You don't know where he comes from, but he opened my eyes! We know that God doesn't pay any attention to sinners, but listens to people who obey him. Ever since the world began, no one has ever heard of anyone giving sight to a person born blind. If this man weren't from God, he wouldn't be able to do such a thing."

"What!" said the Pharisees. "Are you trying to teach us, you miserable sinner? You've been a sinner ever since you were born!" And they threw him out.

When Jesus heard that the Pharisees had thrown the man out, he found him and said, "Do you believe in the Son of Man?"

"Sir," said the man, "who is he? Tell me, so I can believe in him."

"You've seen him," said Jesus. "He is speaking to you."

"Lord, I do believe!" said the man, and he bowed down and worshiped him.

Jesus said, "I came into this world so the blind would see and those who see would become blind. I don't judge them. They judge themselves when they reject me."

He said this because the man who had been blind now believed in him, while the Pharisees' hearts were becoming harder and harder.

"Surely," said the Pharisees, when they heard him say this, "we're not blind!"

"If you were blind," said Jesus, "you wouldn't be guilty of sin, but since you say you can see, you're guilty."

These religious leaders didn't care for the people as Jesus did. Jesus said to them, "I am the good shepherd. The good shepherd lays down his life for the sheep. The hired man leaves the sheep and runs away as soon as a wolf comes. He works for pay and he doesn't care about the sheep.

"I am the good shepherd. I know my sheep and they know me, just as I know the Father and he knows me. I lay down my life for my sheep, as the Father commands me."

When the Pharisees heard this, they said, "He's out of his mind! Don't pay any attention to him."

But some of them said, "A man possessed by a demon couldn't open the eyes of the blind."

Then they gathered around Jesus and demanded, "Why are you making us hold our breath in suspense? If you're really the Messiah, tell us in plain words."

"I've told you, but you don't believe me," said Jesus. "The works I do in my Father's name give witness to me, but you refuse to believe."

Then he said, "My Father and I are one."

They picked up stones to kill him for saying this.

"I've done many good works for you to see," he said. "Works from my Father. Which of these are you stoning me for?"

They answered, "We're not stoning you for doing any good work, but for committing the crime of blasphemy. You're just a man, and you claim to be God!"

They tried to grab him, but before they could hurt him, he slipped away.

27

Some Surprising Teaching

Matthew 8, 11; Luke 9-10, 14

ON THE way back to Galilee, Jesus and his disciples came to a village where a woman named Martha welcomed him into her house. Martha had a sister named Mary, who sat at Jesus' feet and listened to his teaching. Martha kept busy serving Jesus and his disciples.

"Lord," she said to him, "don't you care that my sister has left me to do all the work by myself? Please tell her to come and help me."

"Martha, Martha," he answered. "You worry and fret about so many things, but only one thing is needed. Mary has chosen the right thing, and it won't be taken from her."

This was a surprising remark for a Jewish rabbi to say, because women weren't encouraged to stop doing housework and listen to religious teaching. But Jesus was full of surprises.

After Jesus and his disciples were back in Galilee, he announced to them that he was returning to Jerusalem. The time was coming for him to be taken up to heaven, and he made up his mind to go to Jerusalem.

He sent messengers ahead of him to make arrangements. They came to a village of Samaritans, but the Samaritans wouldn't welcome Jesus, because he was on his way to Jerusalem.

When James and John heard about this, they said, "Lord, do you want us to call down fire from heaven to burn these people up?"

Jesus answered, "You don't know what spirit you belong to! The Son of Man didn't come to destroy lives, but to save them."

Then Jesus and his disciples went on their way. A crowd followed them, and he taught the people as he walked along, speaking to them about the kingdom of God.

A scribe came to him and asked, "Teacher, what are the things that I must do to receive eternal life?"

Jesus said, "What is written in the Law? What do you think the Scriptures say about that?"

The man answered by repeating the teaching of Moses:

> You must love the Lord your God
>   with all your heart,
>   with all your soul,
>   with all your strength,
>   and with all your mind.

Then he added another quote from Moses:

> You must love your neighbor
>   as you love yourself.

"Good!" said Jesus. "You have answered correctly. If you do this, you will live."

But the scribe wanted to show that he was right to ask the question. "Who is my neighbor?" he asked.

Jesus answered by telling the story of "the good Samaritan."

"Once a man was traveling from Jerusalem to Jericho, when he fell into the hands of some robbers. They took everything from him. Then they beat him and left him for dead.

"A priest happened to be going down that same road. When he saw the man, he passed by on the other side.

"Another religious leader, a Levite, also came to that place and saw the man and passed by on the other side.

"But a Samaritan who was on a journey came

upon the injured man. When he saw him, he felt
pity for him. He went over and bandaged his
wounds. Then he set the man on his own animal,
led him to an inn, and took care of him there.

"The next day he took out two pieces of silver
and gave them to the innkeeper and said, 'Look
after him. On my way back I'll pay any extra I
owe.'

"Now," said Jesus to the scribe, "which of these
three, do you think, was a neighbor to the man
who fell into the hands of the robbers?"

"The one who showed loving-kindness," he
answered.

Jesus said, "Go and do the same."

28

Looking for the Lost

Matthew 15; Luke 15

ON THE way to Jerusalem, Jesus told the people three stories about God's love for sinners.

"Suppose," he said, "that one of you had a hundred sheep and lost one of them. Wouldn't you leave the ninety-nine in the pasture and go look for the lost sheep until you found it? And when you found it, wouldn't you gladly lift it onto your shoulders and carry it back home? Then wouldn't you call your friends and neighbors together and say to them, 'Come and celebrate with me, for I've found my lost sheep'?

"In the same way, I tell you, there will be more joy in heaven over one sinner who turns to God than over ninety-nine nice people who stay just as they are."

Then Jesus said, "Suppose a woman has ten silver coins and she loses one. Won't she light a lamp and sweep the house and look carefully until she finds it? And when she finds it, won't she call together her friends and neighbors and say to them, 'Come and celebrate with me, because I've found the silver coin I lost'?

"In the same way, I tell you, there's joy among the angels of God over one sinner who repents."

Then Jesus told the story of "the prodigal son," about a father's love for his lost child.

"Once there was a man who had two sons. The younger one said to him, 'Father, give me my share of the property now.' So the man divided his property between his two sons.

"Soon afterward the younger son sold his share and took the money and went to a foreign country, where he wasted all that he had on a life of sin. When he ran out of money, there was a severe famine in the country, and he had nothing to eat. So he went to work for one of the local men, who sent him out to his farm to feed the pigs. He wished he could eat the leftovers that were given to the pigs, but no one would give him a thing.

"Finally he realized how stupid he was acting, and he said to himself, 'All the people who work

for my father have more food than they need, and here I am, dying of hunger! I'll leave this place and go to my father and say, "Father, I've sinned against God and against you. I no longer deserve to be called your son. Treat me like one of your servants." ' Then he got up and went back to his father.

"While he was still a long way off, his father saw him and had pity on him. He ran to meet him and threw his arms around him and kissed him.

" 'Father,' said the son, 'I have sinned against God and against you. I no longer deserve to be called your son.'

"But the father called to his servants, 'Hurry! Bring the best robe and put it on him. Give him a ring for his finger and sandals for his feet. Then go and get the prize calf and butcher it for a great feast. We'll celebrate because this, my son, was dead and has come back to life. He was lost and has been found!'

"They began to celebrate. Meanwhile, the older son was still in the fields. As he was coming home, he heard the sound of music and dancing near the house.

"He called one of the servants and asked, 'What's going on?'

" 'Your brother has come back,' answered the servant, 'and your father has killed the prize calf for a feast, because he found his son, well and safe.'

"The older brother was so angry, he refused to go into the house. His father came out to beg him to enter. But the older brother answered, 'Look, all these years I've worked for you like a slave, and I've never disobeyed your orders. Yet you never even gave me a young goat to celebrate with my friends. But when this son of yours who wasted your money on wild women comes back, you roast the prize calf for him!'

" 'My son,' said the father, 'you're always here with me. Everything I have is yours. But we were right to celebrate and rejoice, for your brother was dead and now he is alive. He was lost and now he has been found!' "

29

How to Enter the Kingdom of God

Matthew 19; Mark 10; Luke 18

IN THIS world, adults are often thought to be more important than children, good people more important than sinners, and rich people more important than poor people.

But Jesus surprised his followers by teaching them that the kingdom of God is different from the kingdoms of this world.

When some parents brought their children to Jesus, the disciples tried to turn them away. Then Jesus called the children to him and said, "Let the little children come to me, and never try to stop them. The kingdom of God belongs to people like this."

Then he hugged the children and laid his hands on them and blessed them.

Another time Jesus told this surprising story:

"Once two men went up to the temple to pray. One man was a Pharisee, and the other was a tax collector.

"The Pharisee stood there and said this prayer to himself: 'I thank you, God, that I'm not like the rest of humanity—robbers, liars, and cheats. I'm not evil and greedy like other people. And I'm especially glad that I'm not like that tax collector over there. I'm not a sinner. I'm a very religious man. I fast twice a week, and God, I give you a tenth of all my income!'

"Meanwhile, the tax collector stood far off. He didn't even raise his eyes to heaven. Instead, he beat his chest in sorrow and prayed, 'God, have mercy on me, a sinner.'

"I tell you," said Jesus, "this man went home right in the eyes of God, but the Pharisee didn't. All who raise themselves up will be humbled, and all who humble themselves will be lifted up."

As he was going to Jerusalem, a man from one of the ruling families came to Jesus and asked him a question. "Good teacher," he said, "what must I do to receive eternal life?"

Jesus answered, "Why do you call me good? Only God is good." Then he said, "You know the commandments:

You must not kill.
You must not steal.
You must not accuse anyone falsely.
You must not commit adultery.
You must honor your father and mother."

"But, Teacher," said the rich young man, "I have obeyed all these commandments since I was a child."

Jesus looked straight at him and said, "There is one more thing you need to do. Go and sell everything you have and give the money to the poor, and you'll have treasure in heaven. Then come back and follow me."

But when he heard these words, the young man's face fell and he looked terribly sad. He went away discouraged, for he was very rich.

Jesus looked around at his disciples and said to them, "How hard it is for rich people to enter the kingdom of God!"

The disciples were amazed at this teaching, but Jesus insisted. "My children," he said, "it would be easier for a camel to squeeze through the eye of a needle than for a rich person to enter the kingdom of God."

The disciples were shocked. "Then who can be saved?" they asked.

Jesus looked into their faces and said, "For human beings this is impossible, but not for God. For God everything is possible."

"What about us?" asked Peter. "We've left everything to follow you."

"I tell you the truth," answered Jesus. "Everyone who has left home and wife and brothers, parents and children, for the sake of the kingdom, will receive a hundred times as much in this age—with persecution—and in the age to come, eternal life.

"In the age to come, when everything is made new, the Son of Man will sit on his glorious throne and my followers will sit on twelve thrones, judging the twelve tribes of Israel."

Then he added, "But many who are now first will be last, and many who are now last will be first."

30

How to Be Great in the Kingdom

Matthew 20; Mark 10; Luke 18—19

AS JESUS and his disciples were walking to Jerusalem, he spoke to them for the third time about his death.

"Listen!" he said. "Now we're going up to Jerusalem, and everything that has been written by the prophets about the Son of Man will come true.

"The Son of Man will be handed over to the chief priests and the scribes. They'll condemn him to death and hand him over to the pagans to be mocked and insulted and spat on. They'll whip him and put him to death. On the third day he'll rise again."

The disciples had no idea what Jesus was talking about. The meaning was hidden from them. But they remembered what he said about twelve thrones, and they knew he was setting up his kingdom.

Then James and John came to Jesus with their mother, and she bowed low before him.

"What do you want?" he asked her.

She answered, "Promise that when you sit on your throne in your glorious kingdom, you'll let my two sons be seated beside you, in the places of honor, one on your right hand and one on your left."

"You don't know what you're asking!" said Jesus.

Then he turned to James and John and asked them, "Can you drink the cup of suffering that I must drink? Can you go through the baptism I must suffer?"

"We can," they answered.

"All right," said Jesus. "You'll drink the cup that I must drink, and you'll be baptized with the baptism that I must suffer. But as for sitting on my right hand and my left—that's not for me to say. Those places belong to the ones whom God has chosen."

When the other disciples heard what James and John were asking, they were very angry. So Jesus called them together and said, "You know

that the rulers of the pagans lord it over them. Their great men have absolute power over them. This must not happen among you!

"Instead, among you, whoever wants to be great must be the servant of all. Whoever wants to be first must wait on the others. For the Son of Man hasn't come to be served, but to serve, and to give his life as a ransom for many."

Then Jesus and his disciples reached the town of Jericho. A large crowd was following them.

As Jesus was passing through the town, a man named Zacchaeus appeared. He was the chief tax collector there and a very rich man. He was eager to see Jesus, but he was so short, he couldn't see over the heads of the crowd. He ran ahead and climbed a sycamore tree so that he could see Jesus as he passed that way.

When Jesus came to the tree, he looked up and said, "Zacchaeus, hurry and come down, for I must stay at your house today."

Zacchaeus hurried down and welcomed Jesus joyfully.

But the people in the crowd were annoyed, and they complained to each other about Jesus.

"He has gone to stay with a sinner," they said. They looked down on sinners like Zacchaeus, and they didn't want Jesus to have anything to do with him.

But Zacchaeus just stood there and said, "Look, Lord, I'm going to give half of what I own to the poor. If I have cheated anyone, I'll pay him back four times as much!"

Jesus said, "Salvation has come to this family today! Zacchaeus, too, is a child of Abraham. The Son of Man has come to seek and find the lost."

31

The Raising of Lazarus

John 11

THERE was a man named Lazarus who was sick. He lived in the village of Bethany, near Jerusalem, with his two sisters, Mary and Martha. The two sisters knew that Jesus was on the way to Jerusalem, and they sent him a message.

"Lord," they said, "your friend is very sick."

But when Jesus received the message, he said, "This illness won't end in death. It will show the power of God, revealing his glory and the glory of the Son of Man."

Jesus loved Mary and Martha and Lazarus very much, but he stayed where he was for two more days. Finally, he said to his disciples, "Let's go."

He explained to them, "Our friend Lazarus has fallen asleep, and I'm going to wake him up."

"Lord," said the disciples, "if he has fallen asleep, then he'll be all right." Jesus was referring to Lazarus' death, but they thought he was talking about natural sleep.

Finally, he told them plainly, "Lazarus is dead. For your sake, I'm glad I wasn't there, because now you'll believe. Let's go to him!"

"Yes," said Thomas to the other disciples, "let's all go and die with him!" He knew how dangerous it was for Jesus to go so near to Jerusalem.

When Jesus arrived, he found that Lazarus had been in the tomb for four days already. Bethany was only about two miles from Jerusalem, and many people had come out to comfort Mary and Martha. When Martha heard that Jesus was coming, she went to meet him. Mary sat quietly in the house.

"Lord," said Martha, "if you'd been here, my brother wouldn't have died. Even now, I'm sure that whatever you ask of God, he will give you."

"Your brother will rise again," said Jesus.

"I know he'll rise again," said Martha. "Everyone will rise in the resurrection on the last day."

Jesus said to her, "I am the resurrection.

Whoever believes in me, even if he dies, will come to life. Whoever is alive and believes in me won't die at all. Do you believe this?"

"Yes, Lord," she said. "I believe that you are the Messiah, the Son of God, the one who is to come into this world."

Then Martha went to the house to get Mary. "The Teacher's here," she whispered. "He's asking for you."

As soon as she heard this, Mary got up and hurried out to meet him. Jesus had not yet entered the village, but was still at the place where Martha had met him. The people inside who were comforting Mary saw her get up quickly, and they followed her. They thought she was going to the tomb to cry.

When Mary came to the place where Jesus was, she fell at his feet and said, "Lord, if you'd been here, my brother wouldn't have died."

Jesus saw her crying and the people with her crying, and he trembled with deep feeling. "Where have you laid him?" he asked.

"Lord," they said, "come and see."

Jesus began to cry.

"How he loved Lazarus!" the people said.

But others said, "He opened the eyes of the blind man. Couldn't he have prevented this man's death?"

Jesus was trembling again as he reached the tomb. It was a cave with a stone laid across the entrance.

"Take away the stone," Jesus said.

"Lord!" cried Martha. "This is the fourth day. By now there will be a smell!"

Jesus said, "Didn't I tell you that if you believe, you'll see the glory of God?"

They took away the stone.

Then Jesus looked up and said, "Father, I thank you for hearing my prayer. Indeed, I know that you always hear me, but I say this because of the people standing around me, so they may believe that you sent me."

After he said this, Jesus shouted in a loud voice, "Lazarus! Come out!"

The dead man came out. His hands and feet

were still tied with linen strips, and his face was still wrapped in a cloth.

"Untie him," said Jesus. "Let him go free."

Many of the people who had been visiting Mary to comfort her saw what Jesus did, and they believed in him. But some others went to the Pharisees and informed them what was going on. The chief priests and the Pharisees had given orders that anyone who knew where Jesus was must inform them, so they could arrest him.

32

The Coming of the Anointed King

John 11—12

THE chief priests and the scribes were gathered together in the ruling council of the Jews. They were very upset.

"What are we going to do now that this man is working all these miracles?" they said.

"If we let him go on like this, everyone will believe in him. Then the Romans will come and take away our temple and destroy our nation!"

Caiaphas, who was high priest that year, said, "You don't understand what's at stake! Don't you realize that it's better for us if one man dies for

the people, rather than the whole nation being destroyed?"

Caiaphas didn't know it, but he was speaking a prophecy. And from that day on, they plotted to kill Jesus.

It was almost Passover time, and many of the country people went up to Jerusalem for the feast. They were looking for Jesus, and they talked about him as they stood around in the temple area.

"What do you think?" they asked each other. "Will he come to Jerusalem for Passover?"

They were curious about Jesus and wanted to see him and Lazarus, because they had heard how Jesus had raised Lazarus from the dead.

The chief priests wanted to see Lazarus, too—to kill him, because what had happened to Lazarus was leading the people to believe in Jesus.

The Pharisees were disgusted at the way the crowds were looking for Jesus. They were afraid of him, and jealous.

When Jesus entered Jerusalem, a great crowd came to meet him, and the Pharisees said, "There's nothing we can do! See—the whole world's following him!"

Jesus knew that they were plotting to arrest him and kill him. He didn't want to die. "My soul is troubled," he told his disciples. "But how can I ask my heavenly Father to save me from this? This is why he sent me into the world."

Then he prayed, "Father, show the glory of your power!"

A voice came from heaven, saying, "I have shown my glory, and I will show it again."

When the people heard the sound of the voice, some said it was thunder.

"No," said others. "It was an angel speaking to him."

Jesus said to them, "This voice came for your sake. The day of judgment has come. The prince of this world will be driven out. And when I am lifted up from the earth, I will draw the whole creation to me."

He was speaking about the kind of death he would suffer, but they didn't understand.

"What's he talking about?" they asked each other. "What does he mean by 'lifted up'? Who is this Son of Man?"

In spite of his teaching and all the miracles he had worked, the people didn't believe in him, and the ones who did believe in him were afraid.

Jesus said to them, "Whoever believes in me believes in the one who sent me. Whoever looks at me sees the one who sent me. My teaching comes from the Father, and whoever accepts it will have eternal life."

Jesus knew that God was working out his plan, that God's promises were coming true in a wonderful and surprising way.

"I tell you the truth," he said to his disciples, "unless the grain of wheat falls into the ground and dies, it is just one grain. But if it dies, it will produce a great new harvest."

They didn't understand. He was God's anointed king, but only later, after he suffered and died and rose again, did they recognize who he really was.

THE WORLD OF JESUS' DAY

•Sidon

•Damascus

Syria

•Zarephath

•Caesarea Philippi

• Tyre

Phoenicia

Iturea

Capernaum• •Bethsaida

Cana• Magdala•

*Mount Carmel   Tiberius   *Sea of Galilee*

Galilee

•Nazareth

•Gadara

Nain•

Region of Ten Greek Cities (Decapolis)

•Caesarea   Aenon•

Mount Ebal *
            •Sychar
         *
Mount Gerizim

Mediterranean Sea

Samaria   **Perea**

Judea   Jericho•   •Bethany-beyond-Jordan

Jerusalem• •Bethany

Bethlehem•

•Hebron

Jordan River

Dead Sea

•Gaza

Idumea

Egypt

Nabatea

Eve Bowers MacMaster graduated from the Pennsylvania State University and George Washington University. She also studied at Harvard University and Eastern Mennonite Seminary. She has taught in the Bible department at Eastern Mennonite College and in the history department at James Madison University, both located in Harrisonburg, Virginia.

Eve visited many of the places mentioned in the Bible while she was serving as a Peace Corps Volunteer in Turkey.

Eve and her husband, Richard, live at Bluffton, Ohio, with their children, Sam, Tom, and Sarah.